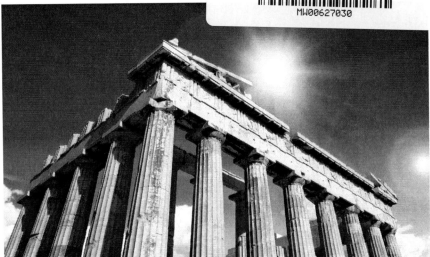

PHILOSOPHY
101

The "BIG IDEA" for the
101 Most Important People
and Concepts in Philosophy

MICHAEL J. VLACH, PH.D.

LAMPION
Press

SILVERTON, OR

PHILOSOPHY
101

Philosophy 101
Copyright © 2016 Michael J. Vlach
All rights reserved.

Lampion Press, LLC
P. O. Box 932
Silverton, OR 97381

ISBN: 978-1-942614-16-6

Library of Congress Control Number: 2016936170

Formatting and cover design by Amy Cole, JPL Design Solutions

Printed in the United States of America

To my wonderful mother, Patricia Vlach,
whose unconditional love has meant so much
to me at every stage of my life.

CONTENTS

INTRODUCTION

"The unexamined life is not worth living."
--Socrates

Studying philosophy can be an intimidating endeavor, especially for the beginner. Complicated ideas from philosophers who lived hundreds and even thousands of years ago can make learning philosophy seem like an impossible task. One can easily become lost in a labyrinth of technical terms and abstract concepts. For many, the more one enters the maze of philosophy, the more lost one becomes. Even philosophy books that are meant for "dummies" can make you feel like a dummy when you are not able to follow long, drawn out explanations of matters. There has got to be an easier way!

As a philosophy teacher, I wanted a tool that would make the discipline of philosophy more understandable and even enjoyable for my students. I wanted a clear and succinct guide that would help beginning philosophy students grasp the essential concepts in philosophy. This book is the result of this desire. If you are interested in studying philosophy, there are three reasons why this book will be of help to you:

First, as the title of this book indicates, this work lays out the 101 most important people and concepts in philosophy. Philosophy is a huge discipline with thousands of people and ideas that could be mentioned. I, though, have zoomed in on those concepts that are most necessary for a basic understanding of philosophy. While no two philosophers would ever completely agree on what should be included in a list of 101 philosophy ideas, I am confident that the entries in this book represent the topics that are most discussed in discussions of philosophy at the beginning level.

Second, this book gives you the information you need in a concise and nontechnical manner. Most entries are only a few pages long, so you will find what you are looking for quickly and avoid long, drawn out explanations. With the exception of those topics that transcend a specific beginning point, most entries are listed in chronological order. Plus, I offer nontechnical explanations that are easy to understand. This book also provides interesting and even goofy information about some of the most important people in the history of philosophy. So not only will you learn a lot, sometimes you may even chuckle. In addition, words highlighted in bold mean that there is another entry in the book devoted specifically to that person or concept.

Third, this work offers "Big Idea" summaries at the beginning of each entry. The "Big Idea" is a one-sentence statement that captures the most important idea of each philosophical topic. With the "Big Idea" you do not have to wade through pages of technical jargon to find what you are looking for. The essential meaning is right there!

Whom is this book for? I have purposely made it for the beginning student of philosophy who wants a basic explanation of the most important ideas in philosophy. To use a baseball analogy, it gets you to first base on the topic at hand.

You can use this book as a reference tool to look up key ideas, or you can read it straight through. Either way, it will give you the information you need to gain a basic understanding of philosophy—a "Philosophy 101" education.

May you find *Philosophy 101: The "Big Idea" for the 101 Most Important People and Concepts in Philosophy* to be of help to you.

1

PHILOSOPHY

BIG IDEA:

Philosophy is the attempt to think rationally and critically about the most important matters in life.

The word "philosophy" was used by the Greek thinker, **Pythagoras**, around 600 B.C. It comes from two Greek terms: *phileo* means "to love" and *sophia* means "wisdom." Philosophy, therefore, is the "love of wisdom." Some have said that philosophy is merely "thinking about thinking." A more formal definition is this: "Philosophy is the attempt to think rationally and critically about the most important matters." In the eighteenth century, **Immanuel Kant** stated that philosophy addresses three main questions: "What can I know?" "What should I do?" and "What may I hope?" These get at the essence of the meaning of life.

Philosophy is perhaps the broadest discipline of study since it covers nearly everything. The five major branches of philosophy are (1) **metaphysics** (study of reality), (2) **epistemology** (study of knowledge), (3) **ethics** (study of right and wrong), (4) logic (study of reasoning), and (5) **aesthetics** (study of art and beauty). Philosophy also covers several other areas such as **philosophy of religion**, philosophy of education, and philosophy of science. Whenever any discipline is looked at philosophically, it comes under the broad umbrella of philosophy.

Some may wonder whether philosophy is worthy of study. After all, isn't philosophy just a meaningless quibbling over words? Is philosophy really practical? While it is true that much of philosophy can appear meaningless and unpractical, there is value in studying it. First, philosophy deals with the most important questions and issues of life such as, "Why am I here?" "Does this world have a purpose?" "Does God exist?" "Is there life after death?" "What is the basis for right and wrong?" "Why does evil exist?" "What makes a war a just war?" If you have ever wondered about these topics or other issues like them, then you have already engaged in philosophy. Although philosophy can get rather technical at times, it tackles "ultimate issues"—topics that matter the most.

Second, the study of philosophy is important because we are all philosophers in some sense. Whenever we deal with the ultimate issues of life such as the meaning of our lives or how we should act, we engage in philosophy. Even those who don't like to study philosophy or say it is irrelevant have reached this conclusion from a philosophical framework. Aristotle said, "All men by nature desire to know." If that is true, then we are all philosophers to some extent.

A third reason for participating in philosophy is because doing so will sharpen your thinking skills. As you study philosophy, you will engage in and evaluate what others have said about various topics. Sometimes you may say, "That makes sense to me." Or, "That's a really dumb idea. Where in the world did he come up with that?" Sometimes you may say, "I'll have to think about that." Studying philosophy will help you think. Plus, you will learn a lot about some of the most important and interesting people in history. You may not agree with everything everybody says, but even in the act of disagreement you will learn something and become a better thinker. So the study of philosophy is a way to sharpen your own thinking skills.

It's also important to remember that philosophy is an activity. And just like any activity such as bowling or riding a bike, the best way to become better at it is to engage it and work at it. Seriously grapple with philosophical issues. Read the works of philosophers. As you do, you will become a better philosopher.

2

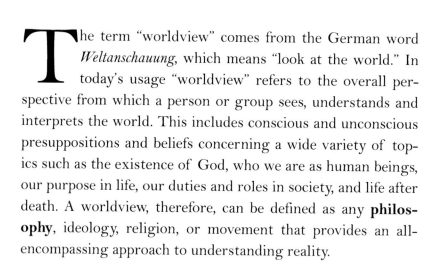

WORLDVIEW

BIG IDEA:

A worldview is the overall perspective by which a person or group interprets and understands the world.

The term "worldview" comes from the German word *Weltanschauung*, which means "look at the world." In today's usage "worldview" refers to the overall perspective from which a person or group sees, understands and interprets the world. This includes conscious and unconscious presuppositions and beliefs concerning a wide variety of topics such as the existence of God, who we are as human beings, our purpose in life, our duties and roles in society, and life after death. A worldview, therefore, can be defined as any **philosophy**, ideology, religion, or movement that provides an all-encompassing approach to understanding reality.

There are several major worldviews today including Christian theism, naturalistic atheism, Eastern pantheism, New Age, Marxism, **nihilism, existentialism,** and **postmodernism.** **Christianity,** for example, promotes a worldview based on the belief that there is a personal and eternal God who created all things for a purpose. Yet because of sin the world is cursed resulting in death. Someday God will restore everything to its intended order. The four key events of the Christian worldview are the (1) Creation, (2) the Fall of Mankind, (3) Redemption in Jesus, and (4) the Restoration of all things with a new heavens and new earth.

Naturalistic atheism, on the other hand, assumes there is no God, the universe happened by chance, and people are the result of an evolutionary process. This naturalistic understanding means that truth and morals are relative and there is no afterlife. People should look to themselves and not some god for meaning.

Eastern religions assume that history operates in a circular manner and that people are reborn again and again in a cycle of reincarnation. This worldview also assumes that attachments and cravings are the main problems in life and that a person should seek to escape these desires and merge into an impersonal Absolute such as Brahman (in Hinduism) or Nirvana (in Buddhism).

Worldviews are not just for philosophers. Every conscious person of age has a worldview whether he or she is aware of it or not. In fact, it is accurate to say that every person thinks and acts in accordance with his or her worldview. What worldview do you live by?

3

METAPHYSICS

BIG IDEA:

Metaphysics is the study of reality and existence.

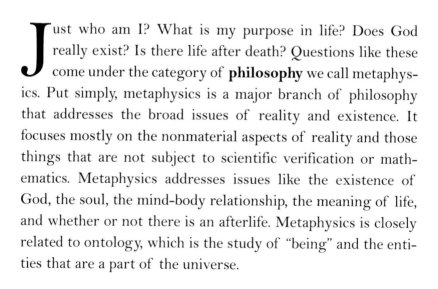

Just who am I? What is my purpose in life? Does God really exist? Is there life after death? Questions like these come under the category of **philosophy** we call metaphysics. Put simply, metaphysics is a major branch of philosophy that addresses the broad issues of reality and existence. It focuses mostly on the nonmaterial aspects of reality and those things that are not subject to scientific verification or mathematics. Metaphysics addresses issues like the existence of God, the soul, the mind-body relationship, the meaning of life, and whether or not there is an afterlife. Metaphysics is closely related to ontology, which is the study of "being" and the entities that are a part of the universe.

Metaphysics comes from two Greek words—*meta*, which means "after," and *physica*, which refers to material reality. The term is said to have originated in Rome in the first century B.C. with the philosopher Andronicus of Rhodes. It quickly came to refer to matters that are "after" or "beyond" material reality.

Most people throughout history have held a view of metaphysics in which there is a nonphysical realm that exists in addition to the physical. **Plato**, for instance, argued that there is a realm of "forms" in another dimension that is more real than the physical realm. He believed that people could not experience true reality without understanding these metaphysical forms. This two-tiered view of reality was quite common in the Medieval Era. **Immanuel Kant**, however, startled many in the eighteenth century when he declared that metaphysical issues like God and the soul were not knowable through reason.

4

EPISTEMOLOGY

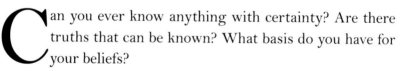

BIG IDEA:

Epistemology is the study of knowledge.

C an you ever know anything with certainty? Are there truths that can be known? What basis do you have for your beliefs?

These important questions are related to the issue of epistemology. Epistemology is the study of knowledge. As one of the major categories of **philosophy**, epistemology addresses the limits of human knowledge including issues such as the definition of knowledge, types of knowledge, the degree to which knowledge is possible, and the relationship between the one knowing and the object being known. Questions such as "How can I know anything?" and "How can I know what is true?" are questions related to epistemology.

Traditionally, there have been two main schools of epistemology. **Rationalism** asserts that the basis for knowledge is the mind and reason apart from prior experience. **Empiricism**, on the other hand, claims that knowledge is rooted in the physical world—in the data collected from our physical senses.

Epistemology has been debated throughout the history of philosophy. In the fourth century B.C., the **Sophists** questioned the idea of knowledge that was certain and universal. **Plato** argued that true knowledge was rooted in "forms" that existed in a different dimension. In the Modern Era, **René Descartes**, **Baruch Spinoza**, and **Gottfried Leibniz** were leaders in promoting rationalism. **John Locke** and **David Hume** promoted empiricism. **Immanuel Kant** attempted to solve the issue by combining elements of rationalism and empiricism.

5

ETHICS

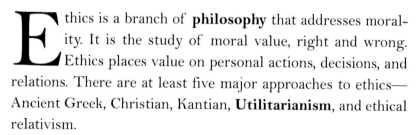

BIG IDEA:

Ethics is the study of morality—right and wrong.

E thics is a branch of **philosophy** that addresses morality. It is the study of moral value, right and wrong. Ethics places value on personal actions, decisions, and relations. There are at least five major approaches to ethics—Ancient Greek, Christian, Kantian, **Utilitarianism**, and ethical relativism.

First, Greek ethics includes the ethical approaches of the ancient Greek philosophers. The **Sophists** in the fifth century B.C. raised questions about what morality really was. Protagoras held that ethics was relative and not anchored in absolute moral truths. **Plato**, though, argued that ethics was rooted in eternal "forms" or "ideas." Thus, there are absolute standards for right and wrong. **Aristotle** argued that virtue is natural and can be cultivated through practice.

Second, Christian ethics is centered in God's will, especially as revealed in the Bible. With this approach, right is what God wills, and wrong is anything against God's will. This is the case because God is holy and good. What is right stems from God's character and is not something outside of God.

Third, Kantian ethics is an ethical approach based on the teachings of the eighteenth-century philosopher **Immanuel Kant**. For Kant, motive is the most important factor, and ethical decisions must be rooted in a "sense of duty," which is a moral oughtness to act in a certain way apart from any feelings or opportunities for reward.

Fourth, Utilitarianism is the view that what is right or good is that which brings the greatest happiness for the most people. Utilitarianism focuses on the potential consequences of actions and claims that decisions should be based on what will bring the greatest happiness for the most people. Jeremy Bentham founded Utilitarianism, and **John Stuart Mill** refined the utilitarian approach that Bentham started.

Fifth, ethical relativism is the perspective that morality and truth are relative to particular societies or individuals. There are no absolute standards for ethics. Moral standards are what people make them to be and can vary widely from culture to culture.

6

AESTHETICS

BIG IDEA:

Aesthetics is the study of art and beauty.

Are there objective or universal standards that determine whether something is art or not? Or are art and beauty purely subjective matters that individuals and societies determine?

Such questions deal directly with the category of **philosophy** called "aesthetics." Aesthetics addresses the issues of art and beauty and matters related to the senses. The term "aesthetics" is related to a Greek term that means "sense perception."

Aesthetics deals with four issues. First, it attempts to define what can be called "art." Second, aesthetics addresses whether something in the areas of literature, painting, music, or architecture can be classified as "good" or "bad." Third, aesthetics ponders the purpose of art. For example, is art merely self-expression or must a creation somehow contribute to society to be considered art? Fourth, aesthetics addresses whether there is some absolute standard for determining and judging art or whether art and beauty are determined by the subjective opinions of a perceiver. The latter perspective is in mind with the old adage—"Beauty is in the eye of the beholder."

In the ancient world, **Plato**, **Aristotle**, and **Plotinus** addressed aesthetical issues. In line with his **theory of "forms"** or "ideas," Plato viewed beauty as an abstract idea that exists outside of our material world. Artists could try to reach "ideal" beauty, but they should know that their creations, no matter how good, were only shadows and imperfect representations of the ideal standards of beauty that existed in another dimension. In his *Republic*, Plato spoke negatively about engaging in the arts since focusing on sensual matters could distract a person from focusing on the more important immaterial forms.

In the Modern Era, **David Hume** argued that art and beauty were related to the human mind when he stated, "Beauty in things exists in the mind which contemplates them." With **Immanuel Kant**, in the eighteenth century, aesthetics was given a distinctive place within philosophy.

Aesthetics has become especially relevant in light of discussions and court rulings in regard to obscenity and pornography. In 1964, Supreme Court Justice Potter Stewart declined to offer a specific definition of hard-core pornography or obscenity but instead declared, "I know it when I see it." In 1972, the U.S. Supreme Court said states could restrict access to "obscene" materials to maintain a decent society. Its ruling raised issues as to what is "obscene" and whether art and obscenity are linked to absolute standards or whether they are merely human constructions.

7

ETHICAL EGOISM

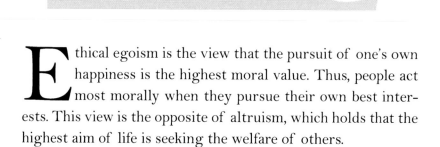

BIG IDEA:

*The pursuit of one's own
happiness is the highest good.*

E thical egoism is the view that the pursuit of one's own happiness is the highest moral value. Thus, people act most morally when they pursue their own best interests. This view is the opposite of altruism, which holds that the highest aim of life is seeking the welfare of others.

While ethical egoism focuses on one's self-interests, it does not necessarily call for rude or overtly selfish behavior. But with all things being equal, a person should look out for his or her own interests over those of others.

Ethical egoism is sometimes viewed as being rooted in psychological egoism, which is the view that people are psychologically oriented toward seeking their own interests above the interests of others. Even if a person appears to act in the best interests of someone else, that act is ultimately motivated by self-interest.

Ethical egoism is found in the person of Glaucon in Plato's *Republic*. Forms of ethical egoism can also be found in the writings of **Aristotle, Thomas Hobbes,** and **Baruch Spinoza**. Modern ethical egoism is often linked with the philosopher Henry Sidgwick and his book, *The Methods of Ethics*, published in 1874. A more recent proponent of ethical egoism was **Ayn Rand**.

8

PHILOSOPHY OF RELIGION

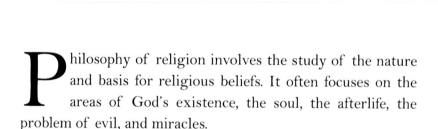

BIG IDEA:

Philosophy of religion examines the nature of, and the basis for, religious beliefs.

Philosophy of religion involves the study of the nature and basis for religious beliefs. It often focuses on the areas of God's existence, the soul, the afterlife, the problem of evil, and miracles.

God's Existence—At the heart of what is called philosophy of religion is the issue of God's existence. **Thomas Aquinas**, for example, promoted the cosmological and teleological arguments for the existence of God. The **cosmological argument** asserts that our world is a contingent thing. Since all contingent beings must have a cause, the world must have been created by God. The **teleological argument** claims that the appearance of design in the universe indicates that there must be a designer who designed the world. **Immanuel Kant** promoted the moral-law argument for God's existence, which asserts that the inner sense of right and wrong within each person is evidence that God exists. **Anselm** promoted the **ontological argument** in which the very idea of God's existence is proof that God exists.

Blaise Pascal offered a different argument now known as **Pascal's Wager**. The Wager states that one is better off believing in God because the consequences of not believing are far worse. If one chooses not to believe in God and is wrong, one will face an eternity in hell. If one chooses to believe in God and he does not exist, then nothing is lost. Thus, it is best to wager one's life on God's existence.

The Soul—Another major subject is the soul. Most religions assert that humans possess an immaterial part called the soul that is the real person. This soul is thought to survive and exist after physical death. **Socrates** and many other ancient Greek philosophers believed in the immortality of the soul. **René Descartes** believed in **dualism**—the view that every person has a soul and a body. Those who hold to a materialist or monistic worldview often deny that there is a soul that is separate from the body.

Problem of Evil—The biggest problem facing religion is the existence of evil in the world. If God is all-powerful and all-good, how can there be tragedies and evil in the world? "**Theodicy**" is a title that describes the attempt to defend traditional views of God in light of evil. Various theodicies have been offered. Irenaeus argued that this present world is a "vale of tears" that prepares us for a coming better world to follow. **Augustine** believed that evil exists because of the free will that

God granted human beings. **Gottfried Leibniz** argued that evil is necessary so that acts of goodness can shine brightest.

Miracles—The major world religions have miracle accounts that allegedly give testimony to the validity of their faiths, but since the **Enlightenment** of the eighteenth century, there has been great skepticism toward miracle accounts. **David Hume** offered the classic refutation of miracles, claiming that a report of a miracle was most likely mistaken. C. S. Lewis (1898–1963) with his work *Miracles: A Preliminary Study* offered a defense of miracles including a rebuttal of the views of those who denied the presence of miracles.

Issues regarding miracles include "How can we know a miracle really happened?" and "If a miracle has occurred, what does that mean for us now?" Most discussions regarding philosophy of religion have centered on Judeo-Christian concepts of God. In recent decades, though, more attention has been given to **Eastern religions** and concepts found within Hinduism and Buddhism.

9

PROBLEM OF EVIL

BIG IDEA:

The presence of evil in the world challenges the existence of an all-powerful and all-good God.

I f God exists, why do bad things happen? Most arguments against God's existence are rebuttals to arguments for the existence of God. One argument, though, that has been used proactively against the idea of God's existence is the problem of evil.

The argument against God's existence from the presence of evil in the world is often stated in the following form: "How can an all-powerful and all-good God allow suffering in the world?" According to the traditional view, God has certain characteristics or attributes. One is that he is "all-powerful," which means he can do whatever he wants. Another is that God is "all-good" and desires what is best for his creatures.

Some believe that these two attributes of God are inconsistent with the presence of evil in the world. Their argument goes like this: "If God is all-powerful and desires the best for his creatures, then why doesn't he prevent evil from happening?" After all, if you had the power to stop a child from being hit by a car, wouldn't you do it? When we look at all the tragedies in the world, we wonder why God does not put an end to these things.

This type of reasoning was offered by the ancient philosopher **Epicurus**, who declared, "If God is not limited in either power or benevolence, why is there evil in the world?" In the nineteenth century, **John Stuart Mill** made a similar declaration: "Not even on the most distorted and contracted theory of good which ever was framed by religious or philosophical fanaticism, can the government of Nature be made to resemble the work of a being at once good and omnipotent."

Many Christian philosophers acknowledge that the problem of evil is a serious issue facing **Christianity**. Some Christians, though, have responded by saying that the very awareness of evil itself is actually evidence for God, for if there is no God there is no rational basis for declaring anything as evil since true evil cannot exist in a random impersonal universe. Good and evil can only exist in the context of persons and relationships. Or to put it in the form of a syllogism:

If evil is real then good must be real.

If good is real then there must be a moral law that is real that is the standard for goodness.

If there is a moral law then there must be a Moral Lawgiver (God) who is the basis for moral law.

Thus, one cannot use "evil" to argue against God since God is the only basis by which the concept of evil can be understood.

Answers to the issue of God's existence in light of evil in the world are often found in the form of a **theodicy**. A "theodicy" is a "justification of God" in light of the presence of evil.

10

DEDUCTION

BIG IDEA:

Deduction is a form of argument in which a conclusion necessarily follows from its premises.

eduction falls within the study of logic. Deductive arguments occur when a conclusion necessarily follows from its premises. The following are examples of deductive arguments:

Premise 1: All dogs have four legs.
Premise 2: Fido is a dog.
Conclusion: Fido has four legs.

Premise 1: All golfers swing a golf club.
Premise 2: Tiger Woods is a golfer.
Conclusion: Tiger Woods swings a golf club.

In both examples above, the conclusions are certain based on their premises. However, two concepts must be considered when dealing with deduction—*validity* and *soundness.*

If an argument is structured in such a way that the conclusion is certain based on its premises, we say this argument is *valid* whether the premises correspond to reality or not. However, in order for a conclusion to be *sound,* both premises must actually correspond to reality. For instance, the second example above is both valid and sound. It is *valid* because the conclusion necessarily follows from the premises. If all golfers swing a golf club and Tiger Woods is a golfer, then it must follow with certainty that Tiger Woods swings a golf club. The conclusion is also *sound* since both Premise 1 and Premise 2 correspond to reality.

The following is a deductive argument that is valid but *not* sound:

Premise 1: All cats have three legs.
Premise 2: Fluffy is a cat.
Conclusion: Fluffy has three legs.

In this example, the conclusion necessarily follows from the premises; thus, it is a valid argument. However, this conclusion is not true since Premise 1 is not true. It is not true that every cat has three legs—most have four. So although this argument is *valid* because the conclusion necessarily follows from its premises, it is *unsound* because Premise 1 does not correspond to reality.

Deductive arguments are often looked to with favorability because they offer certainty. One limiting aspect of deductive arguments, though, is that they do not produce any new knowledge and they appear to codify what we already know.

11

INDUCTION

BIG IDEA:

Induction involves general conclusions based on observations and experiments.

In the area of logic there is a category of argumentation called induction. Induction involves conclusions based on observations and experiments.

For example, imagine a man who travels the world to observe all the swans he can find. After evaluating ten thousand swans, all of which were white, he concludes that "all swans are white." This conclusion that all swans are white would be an inductive argument since it is based on a specific number of observations.

Imagine another example. Suppose a woman observes one hundred trees in Nebraska over a period of thirty years. She observes that every September all the trees begin to lose their leaves. She thus concludes that "all trees in Nebraska begin to lose their leaves in September." This, too, would be an inductive argument since the conclusion was based on repeated observations.

Induction is the basis for science. Scientists observe and test certain phenomena and objects and then draw conclusions from their observations. Most people use induction on a regular basis, too, and would have a hard time functioning without it. Induction leads us to believe the sun will rise tomorrow and that the roofs over our heads will not collapse on us. It helps us conclude that the apples we eat from our local grocery store are not poisonous. Induction, though, cannot give us 100 percent certainty. After all, it is possible that tomorrow the sun will not rise, a nonwhite swan will be found, and the next apple we eat from the local grocery store will poison us.

Although induction is a common part of life, **David Hume** was skeptical about induction, claiming that it is based on guessing and not on logical argument. **Karl Popper**, too, warned against trusting in the certainty of induction by stating that future data may render our inductive conclusions of today as false.

12

DUALISM

BIG IDEA:

*Reality consists of two parts—
the physical and the
nonphysical.*

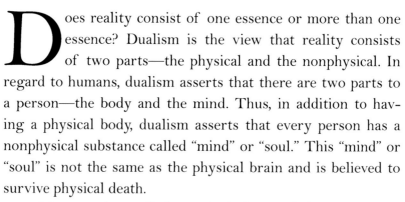

Does reality consist of one essence or more than one essence? Dualism is the view that reality consists of two parts—the physical and the nonphysical. In regard to humans, dualism asserts that there are two parts to a person—the body and the mind. Thus, in addition to having a physical body, dualism asserts that every person has a nonphysical substance called "mind" or "soul." This "mind" or "soul" is not the same as the physical brain and is believed to survive physical death.

Most major religions, including **Christianity** and Hinduism, promote a form of dualism since most of them believe that the soul of a person survives physical death

(Buddhism, however, does not affirm an eternal soul). **Socrates** promoted a form of dualism when he argued for the immortality of the soul after physical death. **René Descartes** also promoted dualism from a philosophical perspective and claimed that the body and soul are distinct but closely related. His form of dualism is referred to as "Cartesian Dualism." Gilbert Ryle mocked dualism, referring to this perspective as the "ghost in the machine" theory.

Monism, on the other hand, is the view that all reality is made of one substance; thus, there is only one level of reality. **Baruch Spinoza** was one of the most famous promoters of monism.

Within the realm of theology, dualism can also refer to the concept that the world is ruled by two opposite and equal forces of good and evil. The religion of Zoroastrianism and some Native American and African tribal groups are viewed as being dualistic in this sense.

13

DETERMINISM / FREE WILL

BIG IDEA:

Determinism holds that all human thoughts and actions are determined by outside factors such as genetics and environment; free will asserts that human choices are free.

Are humans free to choose how they will act or are their actions determined by other factors beyond their control? Two perspectives that attempt to answer this question are determinism and free will.

Determinism is the view that all events and actions in the universe are the effects of other causes. Thus, every event has a cause that makes it inevitable. For example, many believe that the laws of physics show that our universe is operating in a mechanical way so that the world must act as it does.

In regard to humans, determinism is the view that the choices, thoughts, and actions of all people are determined by causes and factors of which a person has no control. For example, when you ate cereal this morning, the reason you did so was because of factors beyond your control and not because you freely chose to eat cereal.

The two primary causes of human behavior believed to influence people are genetics and environment. Determinism can take a religious form, too, as some believe that God predetermines everything that happens. Some stronger forms of Calvinism, for example, assert that God's decrees and predestination plan determine all actions and events in the universe including the deeds of humans.

An extreme form of determinism called "hard determinism" holds that no human thoughts and actions are ever truly free since they are all determined by genetic makeup and environmental factors. Because no actions are free, no person can truly be held accountable or responsible for acting as he or she did. Nor can someone truly be told, "You should have acted otherwise."

Hard determinism appears to challenge traditional views concerning morality and responsibility. If people only think and act as they do because of factors beyond their control, then in what sense can people be held morally responsible for their actions? Most people believe that humans can only be held accountable for actions that they were truly free to make. If a murderer had no real choice but to kill his neighbor, how can we hold the murderer responsible for his actions?

Critics of hard determinism claim that this view not only destroys morality and responsibility, it also undermines the importance of relationships. It affects how one views the future since the hard determinist view believes the future to be as fixed as the past.

Another form of determinism is "soft determinism." This perspective asserts that all human actions are determined, but it differs from hard determinism in claiming that there is a sense in which humans are free to make certain choices. Freedom, though, is redefined to include those actions a person volitionally wanted to commit; a non-free action would be a coerced action. According to soft determinism, a person can truly be held accountable for those actions he or she wanted to do.

Free will, on the other hand, is the view that human choices are free and not determined solely by other factors. Although genetics and environment play into how a person will think or act, a person has the ability to rise above these factors and choose which option he or she will do. Thus, free will is the real ability to choose between two or more different options. Those who hold this view of free will are often called libertarians. Some who believe in free will assert that the immaterial part of a person—one's soul—is able to rise above factors such as genetics and environment and make truly free choices.

14

NATURALISM

BIG IDEA:

Matter and energy are the only realities; there are no supernatural beings or events.

Naturalism is a **worldview** that assumes that the universe is a closed system in which matter and energy are the only realities. This perspective rules out the existence of any supernatural beings—including God, gods, angels, devils, and various other supernatural or preternatural beings such as ghosts, goblins, and poltergeists—and any supernatural activities. According to naturalism, the world operates according to natural laws in which there are series of causes and effects. Because the universe operates according to natural processes, there are no miracles or events that have any supernatural causes. Everything in the universe is subject to scientific study and verification.

Naturalism is consistent with materialism—the view that all of reality is inherently connected to the physical realm. Naturalism disagrees with **dualism** and its assertion that reality is made up of two distinct substances—the material and the immaterial. This rejection of dualism means that naturalists do not believe that people have immortal souls that survive physical death. For naturalists, the present life of a person is the only life he or she will ever have. There are no past lives due to reincarnation nor is there a future life in some state of bliss or torment.

Because naturalism rejects any concept of the supernatural, this view is consistent with **atheism**. Naturalism also usually leads to the rejection of moral absolutes since there is no divine being or law that determines what is right and wrong. Thus, naturalism often leads to ethical relativism in which individuals and societies are free to determine their own standards for right and wrong.

David Hume was a key figure in laying a philosophical basis for naturalism. He attempted to refute the presence of miracles, claiming that testimonies of miracles were most likely false reports. Charles Darwin's theory of **evolution** was also important in that it offered a purely naturalistic explanation of origins. Naturalism is well represented today and is a popular worldview in the academic and scientific communities of the Western world.

15

ATHEISM

BIG IDEA:

God does not exist.

D oes God exist? Atheism is the view that there is no God or gods. It actively asserts that the evidence in the world indicates that there is no divine being(s). It is the opposite of theism, which asserts that there is a God or gods. Atheism is also distinct from **agnosticism**, which declares that the evidence is inconclusive as to whether there actually is a God or not.

Followers of atheism are called "atheists." Atheists believe the concept of God is a human construct that has been used throughout human history to serve various psychological and social needs. For example, the idea of God meets the psychological need for some controlling force in the universe that makes sense of life and the unknown. The notion of God has also been used as a unifying factor for some people groups to rally around. Atheists believe that God has served as a convenient explanation for apparently unexplainable happenings. With the rise of science and technology, however, atheists believe that the need for God will decrease as science and reason continue to offer natural explanations for matters once considered unexplainable.

Atheists claim to use rational and natural explanations to explain reality and do not rely on other-worldly explanations for the universe. They have offered several arguments for the nonexistence of God, but most of these have been considered as counterpoints to arguments for the existence of God. One proactive argument offered by atheists, though, is the **problem of evil**. Allegedly, the presence of tragedies and evil in the world show that an all-good and all-powerful God does not exist.

In 1841, **Ludwig Feuerbach** declared that God was a creation of the human mind to help people deal with their fears. Charles Darwin's theory of **evolution** was important to atheism in that it offered a view of the development of species that did not rely upon a divine creator. In the late nineteenth century, **Friedrich Nietzsche** took a strong atheistic approach, arguing that "God is dead" and that the old morality of **Christianity** needed to be replaced with something better for the modern world.

Atheism has always been a minority view, although it has often been well represented. The fall of the Soviet Union, an atheistic state, and the increasing number of Christians and Muslims in several continents has led some to believe that atheism is decreasing in influence. Yet, the early twenty-first century witnessed the rise of a "new atheism" in the works and teaching of men such as Richard Dawkins, Sam Harris, Christopher Hitchens, and Daniel Dennett. These new atheists have not viewed religion as a positive force, but as the cause for much that is wrong in the world.

16

EASTERN RELIGIONS

BIG IDEA:

Life is full of suffering, and the goal of life should be to put aside personal attachments and cravings and reach union with an impersonal Absolute.

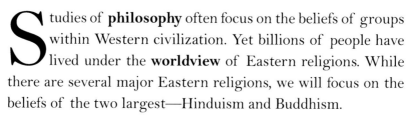

Studies of **philosophy** often focus on the beliefs of groups within Western civilization. Yet billions of people have lived under the **worldview** of Eastern religions. While there are several major Eastern religions, we will focus on the beliefs of the two largest—Hinduism and Buddhism.

There are several core beliefs of Eastern religions like Hinduism and Buddhism. The first is that time and history move in a circular fashion. Much like the seasons of the year, history moves in cycles, not in a linear fashion as Western religions and philosophies have asserted.

A second key belief of Eastern religions is the "cycle of rebirths" or "reincarnation." With this perspective, the current life of a person is not his or her first. In fact, each person alive today has probably experienced many previous lives and will experience more in the future. For example, in a previous life one may have been a bush or a lion or another human being. This cycle of rebirths will continue until a person reaches *moksha* or "liberation" from the cycle of rebirths.

The universal force or law that governs one's cycle of rebirths is *karma*. When people do bad things, they increase their karmic debt and will have a more difficult time reaching liberation. A person who does good and selfless acts will lighten his or her karmic debt and will put him or herself closer to liberation.

A third key belief of Eastern religions is that the Absolute in the universe is mostly impersonal and indescribable. In Hinduism, this Absolute is called Brahman. At times, Brahman may manifest itself in various gods that have personal characteristics, but Brahman cannot be described as possessing human characteristics.

A fourth key belief of Eastern religions is the view that a person's main goal in life should be to rid himself of all cravings and desires and to merge with the Absolute. In Hinduism, the aim is to merge oneself with Brahman. In Buddhism, the goal is to reach Nirvana, a state in which one is free from suffering. Both Brahman and Nirvana are by nature indescribable, and union with them cannot be put into words.

While still a minority in the West, the Eastern **worldview** has been on the rise in the United States since the 1960s.

17

PRE-SOCRATIC PHILOSOPHY

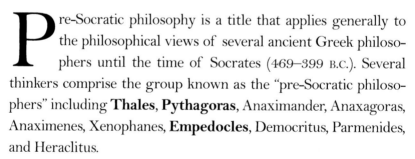

BIG IDEA:

*The pre-Socratic philosophers
inaugurated the era of philosophy
by speculating about what the
world was made of.*

P re-Socratic philosophy is a title that applies generally to
the philosophical views of several ancient Greek philosophers until the time of Socrates (469–399 B.C.). Several
thinkers comprise the group known as the "pre-Socratic philosophers" including **Thales**, **Pythagoras**, Anaximander, Anaxagoras,
Anaximenes, Xenophanes, **Empedocles**, Democritus, Parmenides,
and Heraclitus.

Not satisfied with mythical answers for reality, pre-
Socratic philosophy was concerned with offering rational and
logical explanations concerning what the world was made of

and how it worked. That is why the pre-Socratic philosophers are often referred to as "cosmologists" (*cosmos* means "world").

Thales, for instance, argued that the primary substance of the world was water. Anaximander said it was fire. Anaximenes claimed it was air, and Xenophanes said earth. Empedocles stated that reality consisted of all four elements. Some of the pre-Socratics anticipated future scientific discoveries and theories. Democritus, for example, held that atoms and void were the only two realities. Anaxagoras promoted a view similar to that of the Big Bang theory of today. Anaximander held to a form of **evolution**.

With the exception of Parmenides (b. 515 B.C.), most of the writings of the pre-Socratic philosophers have been lost. Much of what we know about them comes from the writings of **Aristotle**. The pre-Socratics have usually been lumped together as a group, but in the last two centuries, some have emerged as important philosophers in their own right. With the coming of **Socrates** and the **Sophists**, the emphasis in philosophy shifted from cosmology to ethical and social matters.

18

THALES

BIG IDEA:

Water is the basic element of the world.

While some say the same for **Pythagoras**, many scholars assert that Thales (c. 625–546 B.C.), a Greek philosopher from Miletus, was the first true philosopher. Also the first of the pre-Socratic philosophers, Thales was one of the first to ask questions about the structure and nature of the world.

According to Thales, water was the basic element of everything. Some mark this theory as the beginning of scientific thought and philosophy since he tried to understand the nature of the world from the natural realm and not from religion. He also believed in the immortality of the soul.

Thales was recognized as one of the Seven Wise Men of Greece. His knowledge of astronomy is legendary since he accurately predicted a solar eclipse that occurred on May 28, 585 B.C. Thales was also the first Greek to fix the length of the year at 365 days.

Thales made contributions to mathematics, particularly geometry. He used geometry to calculate the heights of pyramids. He also is linked with the Thales' Theorem which states that "if A, B and C are points on a circle where the line AC is a diameter of the circle, then the angle ∠ABC is a right angle." Thus, Thales is the first person to have a mathematical discovery attributed to him. It is believed that Thales offered an ox to the god Apollo as an act of thanksgiving for his discovery.

19

PYTHAGORAS

BIG IDEA:

Mathematics is the ideal expression of reality.

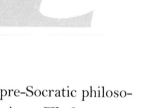

Pythagoras (c. 582–500 B.C.) was a pre-Socratic philosopher. While others say the same about **Thales,** some recognize Pythagoras as the first philosopher.

Pythagoras is also famous for holding that the fundamental principles of the world are mathematical relations. For him, grasping mathematics was necessary for understanding the world. He pioneered the study of geometry, and the Pythagorean Theorem was named after him. Pythagoras taught about the mathematical relationships between notes in the Greek musical scales.

Legend has it that Pythagoras once drowned a student who pointed out the presence of irrational numbers since this threatened the certainty of mathematics.

Pythagoras is also famous for his religious beliefs and actions. He founded a religious community in which vegetarianism was promoted and the eating of beans was prohibited. He also believed that the souls of people could transmigrate to animals at death. Pythagoras took this view so seriously that he once stopped a man from beating a puppy because he thought he heard the voice of a departed friend in the puppy's whimper.

Pythagoras's beliefs on the immortality of the soul would have a big influence on **Plato**. Some assert that Pythagoras's views on mathematics prefigured those of the twentieth-century scientist, Albert Einstein.

20

CONFUCIUS

BIG IDEA:

Humans are good and learn best from a wise and virtuous ruler.

onfucius (551–479 B.C.) was a Chinese sage who set forth a social and political philosophy that would become popular in China and other Asian countries. The name "Confucius" is the Latin translation of "Kung Futzu," which means "Master Futzu."

Confucius was born into a wealthy family during a time of great violence and political upheaval. From an early age he desired to become wise so that he could impact society with his wisdom. To become well-rounded, he studied and practiced archery, music, arithmetic, and calligraphy. At age nineteen, Confucius married and fathered a son and a daughter.

He never held significant positions of power although he served the Duke of Lu for a time. Confucius functioned primarily as a teacher. He attracted three thousand followers with a small number becoming his close disciples.

At the heart of Confucius's philosophy was the concept of *jen*. This word has been translated into English as "good," "benevolence," and "virtue." *Jen* refers to the ideal relationship that should exist between humans. It includes the concepts of gentility, goodness, and benevolence. The ideal man (or *chun-tzu*) who embraces and practices *jen* treats people humanely. Those who practice *jen* will experience a good and happy life. For Confucius, *jen* was not some abstract metaphysical concept but a near reality that could be grasped by the average person.

Confucius believed in the goodness of humans. He also asserted that humans learn best from a good example. Confucius taught that every society needed a good leader, a *junzi*, who would act as a role model for the people. Thus, harmony in society could best be achieved when a society had a good ruler and the people obeyed this leader. Confucius was also a strong believer in education. This contrasted starkly with the competing Chinese philosophy of the time, **Daoism**, which stressed inactivity and noninvolvement with educational and political processes.

Near the time of his death, Confucius was worried that he had little influence upon society. Confucianism, though, gained in popularity and became the official ideology of the Chinese state in the second century B.C. Although primarily a political philosophy, Confucianism is sometimes viewed as a religion as some began to worship Confucius as a deity. Most Chinese scholars, though, consider Confucius to be a great teacher, but they do not worship him. Confucius himself never claimed deity.

The principles of Confucianism are contained in nine ancient Chinese works handed down by Confucius and his followers. One of these, the *Analects*, is the most important text in Confucianism and is the most reliable source of knowledge about Confucius.

Confucianism is no longer the state religion of China since the communist takeover in 1949. Confucianism, however, is experiencing a rebirth in some parts of Asia including Korea, Japan, Taiwan, and Singapore. Clearly, Confucius's concern that he made little impact has proven to be inaccurate.

21

DAOISM

Daoism (or Taoism) is a Chinese philosophical system that began around the sixth century B.C. with the life and teachings of the founder of Daoism—Laozi (or Lao Tzu). Laozi allegedly wrote the *Tao Te Ching* ("The Way and Its Power"), which explains basic Daoist beliefs.

According to Daoism, the absolute or primary concept in the universe is *Dao*. This *Dao* is a mysterious, cosmic power that is present in all experiences. It is an impersonal and invisible way that the universe follows. Indescribable in nature, the *Dao* is a natural force that makes the universe the way it is.

With Daoism, the universe is neither good nor evil—it is beyond good and evil. The universe just is. The secret to living a good and harmonious life is through inactivity. Thus, one of the key concepts of Daoism is *wuwei*, which is the accomplishing of tasks without assertion or aggression.

According to Daoism, active attempts to conquer nature or improve society are futile and only make things worse. Thus, Daoism does not promote advanced education, rituals, and participation in social and political institutions. These things are artificial structures that draw people away from the peace and harmony that come through inaction. Trouble and suffering come when people are too active.

According to Daoism, the best life is the simple life of inactivity and attention to the basic needs of your family. A motto of Daoism could be "Live and let live." By doing nothing, humans can exist in harmony with nature. A long life is often viewed as the reward for those who live in harmony with the *Dao*.

The concepts of "Yin and Yang" come from Daoism. "Yin and Yang" means "shaded" and "sunny" and refers to the opposite and complementary forces in the universe. "Yin" refers to the dark and female aspects of things, and "Yang" represents the light and male aspects of reality. According to Daoism, opposites are identical aspects of the same reality.

The concept of "Feng Shui" is linked also to Daoism. Literally meaning "wind and water," Feng Shui refers to the practice of establishing harmony and juxtaposition with objects such as furniture and buildings. It is thought that the proper positioning of a home, office, or building can positively affect the fortunes of the owner.

Although Daoism is often identified as a religion, it is more appropriately classified as a philosophy since it lacks many of the metaphysical elements of other religions. In fact,

many Daoists have accepted Buddhism as their primary religion. Among the native Chinese, the influence of Daoism has
been second only to that of Confucianism.

22

EMPEDOCLES

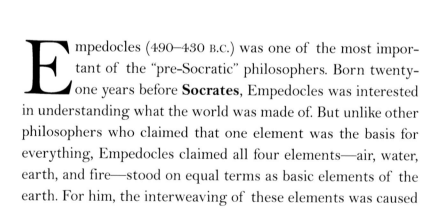

BIG IDEA:

The world is made of four elements—air, water, earth, and fire.

mpedocles (490–430 B.C.) was one of the most important of the "pre-Socratic" philosophers. Born twenty-one years before **Socrates**, Empedocles was interested in understanding what the world was made of. But unlike other philosophers who claimed that one element was the basis for everything, Empedocles claimed all four elements—air, water, earth, and fire—stood on equal terms as basic elements of the earth. For him, the interweaving of these elements was caused by two forces—love and strife.

Empedocles also held to a crude form of evolution in which random chance formed matter into isolated body parts including unsocketed eyes, heads without necks, and arms without shoulders. By chance, these body parts came together and linked into living organisms.

Empedocles believed in the transmigration of souls. In fact, he told his followers to avoid eating animals since their bodies were the dwelling places of punished souls. He believed that he had experienced several past lives himself. Writing in his usual style of poetry, he declared, "I was once in the past a boy, once a girl, once a tree. Once too a bird, once a silent fish in the sea."

Empedocles was an active politician and physician. He used magic and drugs to heal people. It was once reported that he raised a woman to life who had been dead for thirty days. Empedocles had a memorable death as well. Claiming to be a god, he threw himself into the volcano Etna to establish his divinity.

23

SOPHISTS

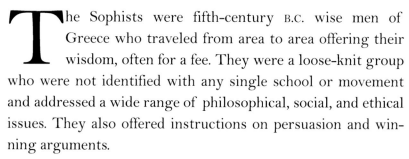

BIG IDEA:

The Sophists were a loose-knit group of philosophers who offered wisdom for a fee.

The Sophists were fifth-century B.C. wise men of Greece who traveled from area to area offering their wisdom, often for a fee. They were a loose-knit group who were not identified with any single school or movement and addressed a wide range of philosophical, social, and ethical issues. They also offered instructions on persuasion and winning arguments.

The Sophists were particularly influential in Athens. Leading fifth-century Sophists include Gorgias, Hippias of Elis, and Prodicus of Ceos. The most famous Sophist was Protagoras. He taught techniques of argument and was especially known for promoting moral relativism. He rejected the concept of absolute universal truth, asserting that morality was relative and created by communities. He coined the famous statement, "Man is the measure of all things."

The original writings of the Sophists are now lost. Our primary source for knowledge about them is **Plato**, who was negative about their ideas and their methods. Plato considered the Sophists to be dishonest since they were more interested in winning arguments than establishing truth and justice. In his writings, Plato depicts **Socrates** as an example of wisdom and virtue who defeats the Sophists and their arguments. **Aristotle**, also, was critical of the relativism of the Sophists.

The term "Sophist" eventually came to have negative overtones. Today, the word "sophistry" refers to false and deceptive reasoning.

24

RELATIVISM

BIG IDEA:

Truth and moral values are not universal and absolute but are determined by the persons and groups holding them.

A re there absolute truths that are true for all people at all times in all places? Or is all truth relative based on the opinions and circumstances of people? Relativism is the perspective that truth and morals are relative to persons and groups holding them; thus, there are no absolute truths or morals that are true for all people at all times. Relativism is the opposite of absolutism, which asserts that there are universal truths and morals that are always true for everyone.

Those who are relativists argue that morality and truth are social inventions. People determine what is right and wrong for them, but their standards are not based in God or on any universal standard. Something is wrong or right, just or unjust, based on what a particular person or society decides.

Relativists often point to differing ethical standards among various ethnic groups and tribes around the world in support of their view. For example, some groups in history condoned polygamy while others only tolerated monogamy.

Since relativists believe that truth and morals are social constructions, they are often opposed to one culture imposing its value system upon another culture. For example, the imposition of **Christianity** upon Native Americans by the European settlers in the seventeenth century is often viewed as wrong by relativists.

Critics of relativism point out that if relativism is accepted, then no society would ever have a right to tell another society that it is wrong, even if the other society condoned genocide, slavery, or domestic abuse. For example, in some Muslim countries women are treated as vastly inferior to men, yet in the West women are viewed as equals to men. So who is to say which culture is more right than the other? Should we say that it is okay for a woman to be mistreated or abused in a Muslim country since that is their culture?

One early relativist was the ancient Greek philosopher Protagoras, who declared, "Man is the measure of all things." In today's postmodern world, relativism is common since **postmodernism** rejects the idea of universal absolute truth.

Some have criticized relativism claiming that it is inherently inconsistent. Critics have said that the act of declaring all truths and morals as relative is itself a universal claim and, thus, internally self-defeating.

25

SOCRATES

BIG IDEA:

*The unexamined life is
not worth living.*

Socrates (469–399 B.C.) is one of the giants of Greek philosophy and is considered by many to be the founder of the Western philosophical tradition. His influence is so significant that the Greek philosophers before him are often lumped together and identified as the "pre-Socratic philosophers."

Socrates wrote nothing himself, and what we know about him comes mostly from his student **Plato**. Socrates' appearance is almost as legendary as his teachings. He was shabbily dressed, barefoot, snub-nosed, and pot-bellied. Physically, Socrates was tough. He served in the heavy infantry of the Athenian army and was known for his courage. Allegedly, he carried out a winter military expedition barefoot.

Early in his career, Socrates had an interesting thing happen to him. An entranced oracle at a shrine in Delphi proclaimed, "None is wiser than Socrates." Socrates was puzzled at this, but he came to believe he was the wisest person because he realized that his wisdom meant nothing. Plato agreed when he paid tribute to his mentor by saying, "That man is wisest who, like Socrates, realizes that his wisdom is worthless."

At age seventy, capital charges were brought against Socrates for introducing strange gods and corrupting the Athenian youth. Socrates was convicted and sentenced to death by drinking hemlock by a slim majority of the 501 judges.

Socrates made several famous statements including "Know Yourself"; "The unexamined life is not worth living"; and "I am not an Athenian or a Greek, but a citizen of the world." For the most part, Socrates stayed away from politics. He believed he was called to pursue **philosophy** and referred to himself as the "gadfly" because like a horsefly on the back of a horse he tried to sting his fellow Athenians into self-examination. He also opposed the **Sophists**, a pragmatic group of philosophers who offered their counseling services for a fee.

Unlike the pre-Socratic philosophers, Socrates did not dwell on what elements the earth consisted of. Instead, he focused mostly on **ethics** and what was right and just. For Socrates, philosophy was a way of life and not just speculation. Moral virtue and knowledge were inseparable; thus, knowledge led to action.

Socrates believed that true knowledge came through dialogue and questioning. He was not content to accept any argument without challenge. For him, unfounded arguments needed to be challenged, and uncritical claims to knowledge should be abandoned. In fact, Socrates is known for founding the "Socratic Method," which features a cross-examination approach to expose false claims to knowledge.

Socrates is also known for the "Socratic Paradox," which is the view that people sin or do the wrong thing because of lack of knowledge. According to Socrates, if people knew the right thing, they would do it because it's in their best interest. Or put another way, "No one does wrong voluntarily."

He also believed in the immortality of the soul. For him, a human being is a soul imprisoned in a body. Food, drink, and sex get in the way of the pursuit of knowledge. The philosopher longs for death so he can finally rid his soul of the carnal body.

Socrates paved the way for the next two great Greek philosophers—**Plato** and **Aristotle**.

26

PLATO

BIG IDEA:

*A more perfect realm
of forms exists outside of
our physical world.*

P lato (c. 427–347 B.C.) stands as one of the most creative and important philosophers in the history of **philosophy**. While certainly an overstatement, it has been
said that the entire enterprise of Western philosophy is really
a series of footnotes to Plato.

A student of **Socrates** and a forerunner of **Aristotle**,
Plato was born into a wealthy family near the end of the
Athenian Empire. Plato's immediate family members were split
over the civil war in 404 that followed the defeat of Athens by
Sparta. In addition to promoting his own significant philosophical views, Plato also wrote down most of what we know about
the life and beliefs of Socrates.

63

Plato founded a school in Athens called The Academy. Several disciplines were studied here, and over the entrance of the school was a statement, "Let No One Ignorant of Geometry Enter." The most famous disciple of this school was Aristotle, who studied at The Academy for twenty years.

A prolific writer, Plato left three categories of writings. The first are the Socratic Dialogues in which Socrates appears in his historical role as one who questions and challenges unfounded ideas. The second category is Socrates as Teacher in which the views of Socrates are expounded. The third is the Later Dialogues in which Plato himself explains his views on matters such as natural science and cosmology. Most of what we know about the man Socrates comes from the pen of Plato.

At the heart of Plato's philosophy was his **theory of forms** (or ideas). In fact, his views on knowledge, **ethics**, psychology, politics, and art are all tied to this theory. According to Plato, there are two realms of reality. First, there is the physical world. Second, there is the world made of eternal perfect "forms" or "ideas." These "forms" are perfect templates that exist somewhere in a different realm and are the ultimate reference points for all objects we see in the physical world. This world of forms is even more real and perfect than our physical world. This view led to a dualism between the spiritual and physical with the former being superior to the latter.

In his *Republic*, Plato wrote one of the greatest works ever on the issue of political philosophy. The *Republic* describes Plato's utopian society—a city with three classes. The first is the Upper Class, which consists of those most fit to rule. This class includes Plato's "philosopher-kings." According to Plato, philosophers possess the most wisdom and, thus, are most qualified to lead society. The second class consists of soldiers, and the third class consists of the workers. In Plato's city, class status is determined at birth; everyone receives an education; women are to be common property; procreation is regulated; and children are brought up by the state. Four virtues are to be emphasized in this city—wisdom, courage, temperance, and justice. Plato's utopian society with strong control by elites and no personal liberties has been picked up by other philosophers including Thomas More (*Utopia*), Thomas Hobbes (*The Leviathan*), and Karl Marx (*The Communist Manifesto*).

Plato's influence was great, and some of his ideas would be picked up centuries later by the last great pagan philosopher, **Plotinus**, and some Christian theologians including **Augustine**.

27

PLATO'S THEORY OF FORMS

BIG IDEA:

Ultimate reality is found in "forms" that are the perfect reference points for things in the physical world.

Plato is one of the most important philosophers in history. At the heart of his **philosophy** is his "theory of forms."

According to Plato, reality consists of two realms. First, there is the physical world—the world that we can observe with our five senses. And second, there is a world made of eternal, perfect "forms" or "ideas."

What are "forms"? Plato says they are perfect templates that exist somewhere in another dimension. These forms are the ultimate reference points for all objects and ideas in our world. They are more real than the physical objects you see in the world. For example, a chair in your house is an inferior copy of a perfect chair that exists somewhere else. A horse you see in a stable is really an imperfect representation of some ideal horse that exists somewhere in another dimension. In both cases, the chair in your house and the horse in the stable are just imperfect representations of the perfect chair and perfect horse that exist in another realm.

According to Plato, whenever you evaluate one thing as "better" than another, you assume that there is an absolute good from which two objects can be compared. For example, how do you know a horse with four legs is better than a horse with three legs? Answer: You intuitively know that "horseness" involves having four legs.

Not all of Plato's contemporaries agreed with Plato. One of his critics said, "I see particular horses, but not horseness." Plato replied sharply by saying, "That is because you have eyes but no intelligence."

Plato used the "analogy of the cave" to illustrate his theory of forms. The analogy goes like this: Imagine several prisoners who have been chained up in a cave for all of their lives, never seeing the outside world. They face a wall in the cave and are never able to face the entrance of the cave. Sometimes animals, birds, people, or other objects pass by the entrance of the cave casting shadows on the wall inside the cave. The prisoners see these shadows on the wall and mistakenly view these shadows as reality.

However, one man breaks free from his chains and runs out of the cave. For the first time, he sees the real world and now knows that the shadows are not reality. He sees real birds and animals, not just shadows of birds and animals. This man is excited about what he sees, and he goes back to his fellow prisoners in the cave to tell them about the real world. But to his astonishment, they don't believe him. In fact, they are angry with him. They say the shadows are reality and that the escaped prisoner is crazy for saying otherwise.

What is the point of this cave analogy? According to Plato, the world outside the cave represents the world of forms while the shadows on the wall represent objects in the physical world. The escape of the prisoner represents philosophical enlightenment and the realization that forms are the true reality. Most people are like the prisoners in the cave. They think the shadows are reality. Philosophers, though, are like the man who escapes the cave and sees the real world. They have true knowledge.

28

BIG IDEA:

Realism asserts that universals exist apart from objects; nominalism claims that universals do not exist apart from objects.

Nominalism and realism are theories related to **episte-mology** (the study of knowledge). Both positions are anchored in their approaches to the concept of **universals**.

Realism is the view that there are universals that are related to but exist apart from thoughts and individual objects in our world. Consider two white horses, for example. Realism asserts that there is a universal concept of "whiteness" of which the two white horses both share. **Plato's theory of forms** is the classic representation of realism. Plato argued that for every object in the physical world, there is a more perfect "form" or "idea" that exists in another realm.

Nominalism, on the other hand, asserts that reality only exists in particular objects. Universals, therefore, have no reality apart from particular things. Thus, there are no concepts like "whiteness" that exist in another dimension. Two objects like horses or rocks may share "whiteness," but this whiteness is located in particular objects and not in some independent concept of "whiteness" that exists somewhere else. Forms of nominalism can be found in the views of **William of Ockham, George Berkeley**, and **David Hume**.

The concepts of nominalism and realism were an important part of medieval philosophy and theology. In general, the time period of 1200–1350 was a period in which realism was accepted. The time period of 1350–1500 was dominated by nominalism.

29

ARISTOTLE

BIG IDEA:

Logic and empiricism are the foundations of knowledge.

Perhaps the most famous figure in the history of **philosophy**, Aristotle (384–322 B.C.), was an influential Greek philosopher who divided philosophy into distinct disciplines. He contributed enormously to a wide variety of philosophical issues such as **aesthetics**, biology, **epistemology**, **ethics**, logic, **metaphysics**, politics, and psychology.

At age seventeen, Aristotle came to Athens from Macedonia to study at Plato's Academy, where he studied for twenty years. Although respectful of **Plato**, Aristotle eventually contradicted important elements of Plato's philosophy. In 342 B.C., Aristotle began tutoring a fourteen-year-old called Alexander, who would later become Alexander the Great. In 335, Aristotle founded his own school in Athens called the Lyceum where he brought together a large group of brilliant research students. In 323, Alexander the Great died, and charges of impiety were brought against Aristotle. To save Athens from "sinning twice" (remember that Athens put **Socrates** to death), he fled the city.

Aristotle wrote a tremendous amount of literature—about 400 books in all (although books back then were often much smaller than books today). Unfortunately, 80 percent of what he wrote has been lost. Still, one million words survived—twice that of Plato's writings.

Aristotle is known as the "father of logic" because he created the syllogism and developed the study of deductive logic. An example of a syllogism that is put in the form of a deductive argument is:

Premise: All men are mortals.
Premise: Socrates is a man.
Conclusion: Socrates is a mortal.

Unlike his predecessor, Plato, who claimed that reality is based primarily in metaphysical "forms" or "ideas" that exist outside of our earthly realm, Aristotle said that reality is based in individual earthly substances. Thus, Aristotle stressed "**universals,**" which for him were common qualities the mind can grasp in the physical world that do not exist independently of the physical world. For example, both rocks and horses can possess the quality of "white," but this does not mean that a concept of "whiteness" exists by itself apart from particular objects. For Aristotle, logic and **empiricism** were the foundation of knowledge.

In the realm of metaphysics, Aristotle is known for his concept of the "Prime Mover." According to Aristotle, all motion is the result of something. Since the universe is in motion, there must be some Prime Mover who caused the universe to function as it does. Although Aristotle's Prime Mover is not the Christian God, Christian philosophers such as **Thomas Aquinas** would claim Aristotle's theory as support for the view that a supreme being caused the world to exist.

In regard to the soul, Aristotle argued that the soul is essentially linked to the body and is not just some spiritual substance that is imprisoned in the body as many Greeks including **Socrates** believed. The function of the soul is to cultivate the intellectual and moral aspects of a person.

Aristotle promoted a virtue theory in regard to ethics. For him, the emphasis in ethics should be on the cultivation of character and becoming a virtuous person. This development takes place over the course of one's life. As he stated, "It is by doing just acts that we become just, by doing temperate acts that we become temperate, by doing courageous acts that we become courageous." For Aristotle, right motive needed to accompany right action in order for an act to be considered virtuous.

Aristotle's influence on the Western world was largely lost with the fall of the Roman Empire. In the ninth century, Arab scholars introduced Aristotle's works to the Islamic world. In the thirteenth century, Christian theologians rediscovered Aristotle. At first, the Catholic Church condemned his works, but scholars from the University of Paris and Thomas Aquinas relied heavily on his writings. Soon Aristotle's works were viewed as the highest achievement of human reason.

30

UNIVERSALS

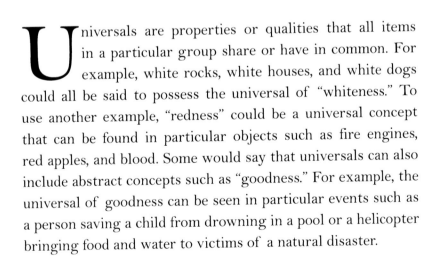

BIG IDEA:

Universals are properties or qualities that all items in a particular group share.

Universals are properties or qualities that all items in a particular group share or have in common. For example, white rocks, white houses, and white dogs could all be said to possess the universal of "whiteness." To use another example, "redness" could be a universal concept that can be found in particular objects such as fire engines, red apples, and blood. Some would say that universals can also include abstract concepts such as "goodness." For example, the universal of goodness can be seen in particular events such as a person saving a child from drowning in a pool or a helicopter bringing food and water to victims of a natural disaster.

Debate continues as to whether universals actually exist apart from particular objects. **Plato** and the Platonic school that followed him believed that universals actually exist apart from any particular manifestations of that universal. For example, the universal of redness exists as an entity itself apart from any particular red objects we see such as fire engines and red apples.

Aristotle, however, argued that universals do not exist outside of particular objects; instead, they exist only in particular things. Thus, Plato would say that "redness" has an existence apart from any examples of "redness" on this earth. Aristotle's view, on the other hand, would say that "redness" does not exist apart from particular objects that are red. Thus, redness is only connected to actual red objects.

31

COSMOLOGICAL ARGUMENT

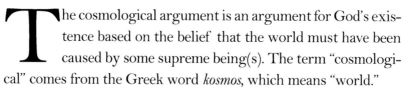

BIG IDEA:

*The world could not exist on its own,
so some intelligent and powerful being
must have caused it to exist.*

The cosmological argument is an argument for God's existence based on the belief that the world must have been caused by some supreme being(s). The term "cosmological" comes from the Greek word *kosmos,* which means "world."

According to the cosmological argument, all contingent things, including our world, must have a cause. But since there cannot be an endless series of causes, or what is called an "infinite regress," there must be one "uncaused cause" that started the process of contingent beings. For **Aristotle**, this ultimate cause of motion or change was the Prime Mover. The Prime Mover caused the motion we now see in the universe.

Christians like Saint **Thomas Aquinas** refined Aristotle's cosmological argument and used it in defense of the Christian God. In short, the cosmological argument, within a Christian context, goes like this: "The world could not exist on its own, so there must have been a first uncaused cause that brought it into being. This uncaused cause is God."

The cosmological argument is still a major argument for the existence of God today. Some have argued against this view, claiming that matter is eternal. Others have said that even if it is true, this argument does not prove the existence of the Christian God. All it shows is that there is some powerful being that created the universe.

The cosmological argument is one of four major arguments for the existence of God along with the **teleological, ontological,** and moral-law arguments.

32

EPICUREANISM

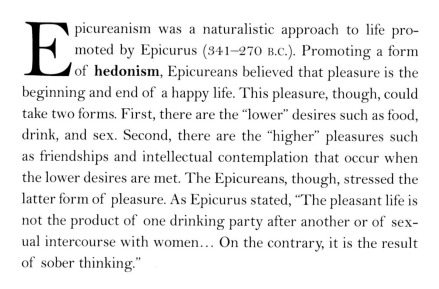

BIG IDEA:

*Pleasure is the beginning
and end of the happy life.*

Epicureanism was a naturalistic approach to life promoted by Epicurus (341–270 B.C.). Promoting a form of **hedonism**, Epicureans believed that pleasure is the beginning and end of a happy life. This pleasure, though, could take two forms. First, there are the "lower" desires such as food, drink, and sex. Second, there are the "higher" pleasures such as friendships and intellectual contemplation that occur when the lower desires are met. The Epicureans, though, stressed the latter form of pleasure. As Epicurus stated, "The pleasant life is not the product of one drinking party after another or of sexual intercourse with women… On the contrary, it is the result of sober thinking."

The Epicureans were known as "garden philosophers" because their instruction often took place in Epicurus's garden at his home. As a place of relaxation from the business of Athens, everyone was welcome to the "Garden" to eat, drink, socialize, and discuss philosophy. Here all people were treated equally including slaves, foreigners, prostitutes, and women.

The Epicureans were not atheists, but they did not believe that gods took an active interest in the world and the affairs of people. They did hold that religion was a barrier to happiness since it fostered a fear of death with all its emphasis on suffering and punishment. Thus, for the Epicureans, happiness involves removing the fear of death and all unnecessary worrying about the afterlife. The terrors of religion are just fairy tales and hindrances to the good life.

After the fifth century A.D., Epicureanism largely died out as Christians disapproved of its anti-supernatural beliefs. Epicureanism was rediscovered in the sixteenth and seventeenth centuries since it appeared consistent with modern science and **humanism**.

33

STOICISM

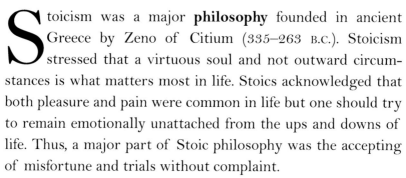

BIG IDEA:

A person should cultivate a virtuous soul and remain emotionally unattached to the ups and downs of life.

S toicism was a major **philosophy** founded in ancient Greece by Zeno of Citium (335–263 B.C.). Stoicism stressed that a virtuous soul and not outward circumstances is what matters most in life. Stoics acknowledged that both pleasure and pain were common in life but one should try to remain emotionally unattached from the ups and downs of life. Thus, a major part of Stoic philosophy was the accepting of misfortune and trials without complaint.

The ideal approach to living was to face life with a grim determination. For example, if a Stoic saw a child drowning, he should do all he could to save the child. But if he failed in his attempt to save the child, he should accept the outcome without feelings of remorse or pity. That is why even today when people face trials with a grim determination, we often hear the statement, "He is stoic."

The Stoics were pantheistic materialists. They assumed that nothing immaterial existed. Thus, all things, including the soul and God, were material objects. Rejecting **Plato**'s dualistic understanding of reality, the Stoics argued for a form of monism in which everything is viewed as existing from one principle.

Stoicism is named after the *Stoa Poikile*, or "Painted Porch," in Athens where the founders of Stoicism taught. In the second and third centuries B.C., Stoicism was popular among many Greeks and Romans and was held by Seneca. The last major figure to promote Stoicism was the Roman Emperor Marcus Aurelius (A.D. 121–180)

34

HEDONISM

BIG IDEA:

The pursuit of pleasure is the highest value.

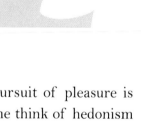

edonism is the view that the pursuit of pleasure is the highest good. Although some think of hedonism as only a philosophy of "Eat, drink, and be merry for tomorrow you die," there are various forms of hedonism.

"Psychological hedonism" holds that people are primarily pain and pleasure beings. Thus, the desire to seek pleasure and avoid pain governs all choices. "Egoistic hedonism" is the perspective that the pursuit of one's own pleasure is the highest good. "Altruistic hedonism" argues that the highest good is the pursuit of the greatest happiness for the greatest number of people.

Hedonism has a long history. Aristippus (c. 430–350 B.C.), a follower of Socrates, was the first to promote a philosophical approach to hedonism. He asserted that people are pain and pleasure beings. They avoid pain and seek pleasure. Thus, the highest good in life is the pursuit of sensual pleasures. The Cyrenaic school, of which Aristippus was the founder, went so far as to claim that pleasure was the only worthwhile pursuit.

The Epicureans, under the guidance of Epicurus (341–270 B.C.), asserted, too, that pleasure is the beginning and end of a happy life. But unlike the Cyrenaics, they claimed there were "higher" pleasures and "lower" pleasures. Lower pleasures were matters like food, drink, and sex. Higher pleasures, though, were things like intellectual contemplation and the cultivation of friendships. For Epicureans, once a person's basic needs of food, drink, and sex were met, people could then focus on the higher pleasures.

Around the eighteenth century, Jeremy Bentham and **John Stuart Mill** promoted **utilitarianism**, which is a social form of hedonism. For Bentham and Mill, the emphasis on pleasure should not stop with the individual; it should be promoted in all of society. Thus, they emphasized the greatest happiness for the most people.

Hedonism has often been criticized as a **worldview**. Some have stated that the exaltation of pleasure as the highest good is unhealthy. Others have stated that pleasure is hard to define and quantify. Plus, what if the pursuit of pleasure leads to conflicts between people?

35

CHRISTIANITY

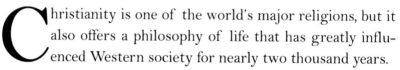

BIG IDEA:

God's program for salvation and restoration is based on the person and work of Jesus Christ.

Christianity is one of the world's major religions, but it also offers a philosophy of life that has greatly influenced Western society for nearly two thousand years.

Christianity was founded by Jesus of Nazareth (c. 4 B.C.– c. A.D. 33), who is famous for his teachings, miracles, death, and resurrection from the dead. The Christian movement was furthered by Paul of Tarsus, who through his missionary travels took Christianity to many areas of the known world.

Much of Judaism is found within Christianity, such as belief in one God and a linear view of history in which God will eventually triumph over evil and establish a new heavens and new earth. Christianity differs from Judaism, though, in its assertion that Jesus was the divine Son of God and the Messiah of Israel. Christianity also uniquely asserts that Jesus' death on the cross was an atonement for the sins of the world. The Christian message is based on four key episodes: the Creation of the world, the Fall of Man, the Incarnation of Jesus, and the Restoration of all things.

While Christianity itself is rooted firmly in the life of Jesus and the writings of both the Old and New Testaments, this religion has often intersected with the discipline of philosophy. Some early Christians rejected any merger between Christianity and philosophy. For example, the church father Tertullian (160–225) declared, "What has Athens to do with Jerusalem?" to show that Greek philosophy had nothing to do with Christianity.

Other church fathers, though, were positive about the value of philosophy. Justin Martyr (c. 100–165), for example, believed that God scattered "the seeds of his Logos [Word]" throughout the world before sending Jesus. Thus, Justin believed that the world had experienced some truths of God through philosophy even before Jesus came into the world. Justin also held that Christianity brought to fulfillment some of the insights of classical philosophy including that of Platonism. Another church father, Clement of Alexandria (150–215), asserted that God gave philosophy to the Greeks in order to prepare them for the coming of Christ. Thus, Greek philosophy was not a competing worldview. According to Clement, Jesus was the fulfillment of philosophy.

The influential theologian and philosopher **Augustine** of Hippo (354–430) also viewed philosophy favorably. Although acknowledging that some areas of philosophy were not valuable, he believed that there was no reason why Christians should not adopt the good things of philosophy and use them in their Christian walk and witness. Augustine himself relied upon several major teachings of **Plato** and **Plotinus** (Plotinus founded **Neo-Platonism**). Augustine credited Neo-Platonism for helping him reject the Manichean view that all reality was material. Augustine also adopted **Plato's theory of forms**, placing these "forms" in the mind of God.

Until the thirteenth century, the Christian church often looked favorably upon the ideas of Plato. During the thirteenth century, though, Christian scholars rediscovered the writings of **Aristotle**. **Thomas Aquinas**, for example, attempted a merger between Aristotelian ideas and Christianity. Aquinas used Aristotle's concept of a Prime Mover as support for his idea that the Christian God must have created and designed the universe.

Christianity is the largest religion in the world with around two billion adherents.

36

NEO-PLATONISM/PLOTINUS

BIG IDEA:

There are three levels of reality—
One, Mind, and Soul.

Neo-Platonism was a complex system for understanding reality that was founded by the Roman philosopher Plotinus (204–270), the last great ancient non-Christian philosopher. Coming more than 600 years after **Plato**, the Egyptian-born Plotinus carried on some of the main ideas of Plato such as: (1) there is an immaterial reality that exists apart from the physical world; (2) a strong distinction exists between an immaterial soul and the physical body; and (3) the immortal soul finds its ultimate fulfillment as it becomes one with an eternal, transcendent realm. Plotinus, though, was not just a mere follower of Platonism. His ideas were novel enough that someday they would come to be known as Neo-Platonism.

Plotinus's works were edited after his death by his disciple, Porphyry. This compilation of writings is called the *Enneads*, which covers a wide variety of philosophical topics including **metaphysics**, **ethics**, logic, **epistemology**, psychology, and physics.

According to Plotinus, the basis of all reality is an immaterial and indescribable reality called the One or the Good. There are several levels of reality that emanate from the One, much like ripples in a pond emanate from a dropped stone. The second level of reality is Mind or Intellect (*nous*). Mind results from the One's reflection upon itself. The level below Mind is Soul. Soul operates in time and space and is actually the creator of time and space. Soul looks in two directions—upward to Mind and downward to Nature, which created the physical world.

According to Plotinus, the lowest level of reality is matter. Thus, matter is viewed very negatively in Neo-Platonism. Plotinus himself held such disgust for physical things that he even despised his own body. For example, he did not celebrate his birthday since the birth of his physical body was nothing to be celebrated. He also did not take care of his physical health or hygiene. Plotinus had pus-filled sores on his body that he refused to care for. Unfortunately for his students, he liked to embrace his pupils, causing many of them to flee from him.

Plotinus's school in Rome did not survive after his death, but his ideas were carried on by his disciples. His ideas had a strong influence on the great Christian philosopher **Augustine**, who adopted several elements of Neo-Platonism. Augustine credited Neo-Platonism for steering him away from the view that all reality is material. Also, Neo-Platonism had an impact on how some Christian doctrines were perceived. The early church's views on God's transcendence paralleled the Neo-Platonic view that the human mind cannot grasp the ultimate reality. Neo-Platonism also heavily contributed to negative views about the physical body and sensual pleasure.

37

AUGUSTINE

BIG IDEA:

*Reason and belief in God
are compatible.*

Saint Augustine (354–430) was the most important philosopher and theologian of the early Christian church era, particularly in the Latin West. The son of a Christian mother and non-Christian father, Augustine admittedly declared that he partook in the lusts of the world as a young man. According to his *Confessions*, he visited prostitutes and took a mistress. Eventually, Augustine converted to **Christianity** and immediately put away his old lifestyle.

In addition to being influenced by the Bible and the beliefs of Christianity, Augustine was impacted by **philosophy**. At age eighteen he gained a love for philosophy and had a special fondness for the works of **Plato** and the ideas of **Stoicism**.

Augustine believed there was compatibility between reason and the Christian faith. In fact, he tried to reconcile faith and reason. For Augustine, belief in the Christian God was the key to understanding reality. Thus, his famous statement, "I believe in order that I may understand."

Augustine Christianized **Plato's theory of forms**, asserting that the perfect eternal "forms" of Plato's theory actually existed in the mind of God (Plato never said where these "forms" existed). Also, like Plato, Augustine said the soul was a higher form of existence than the body.

Unlike Plato, though, Augustine argued that God created the world without using prior existing materials. He also promoted the **teleological argument**—the view that the apparent design of the universe shows that God created it. Augustine also stated that before God created the world, there was no time. Thus, God himself is outside of time. Augustine is also known as the "father of **just war** theory." He said that nations can declare war on other nations that act wickedly. Participation in a just war, though, does not violate the "do not kill" command in the Bible.

Augustine argued that evil in the world comes from our participation in the sin of Adam and Eve. Since Adam was the father of the entire human race, everyone was present in Adam in seed form when Adam sinned.

Augustine was one of the first philosophers to offer a philosophy of history. He promoted a linear view of history in which history has a purpose and is headed toward a divinely appointed completion. In his important work *The City of God*, Augustine said history can be divided into two cities. The earthly city consists of everything that is known by love of self. The city of God, though, consists of everything that is known by love of God. Many of Augustine's views would be adopted by the Roman Catholic Church.

Augustine had enormous intellectual honesty. In his old age he went over all the books he had published and wrote a book called *Retractationes* in which he retracted all things he considered errors.

Augustine's sexual behavior as a young man led to an excessively negative attitude toward sex in general. For example, he believed that it was a venial sin for a married couple to keep having sex when the woman was too old to bear children. He also stated that God designed the reproductive organs to be near the organs that excrete waste to show that they were dirty. Augustine believed that married love was holy for married couples, but his discomfort with sex after his conversion produced anti-sex undertones in the Western church.

38

JUST WAR

BIG IDEA:

*Just war theory addresses
what conditions, if any,
make a war justified.*

Nations have been at war with each other since human civilization began. But what conditions, if any, make a war just? The concept of "just war" is built on the assumption that war is bad and should be avoided, but there also are times when warfare is justified. Just war theories usually address two main areas: First, under what conditions is it right to go to war? And second, what is the moral way to conduct a war?

As for the history of just war theories, the ancient Greeks and Romans discussed the morality of war. Cicero (106–43 B.C.), for instance, argued that there was no acceptable reason for war outside of self-defense, which included the right to defend one's honor. Cicero aside, **Augustine** is often viewed as the "father of just war theory." Augustine was against individuals retaliating when injured, but he believed that nations had the right to defend their citizens and keep the peace. For Augustine, the primary purpose of a just war was to reestablish peace.

Centuries later, **Thomas Aquinas** developed the concept of just war. He asserted that three things were necessary for a war to be just: (1) the one declaring a war must be a rightful sovereign, a legitimate leader; (2) the nation being attacked must deserve it because of some serious fault or injustice; and (3) the nation doing the attacking must have a good intention such as advancing good or stopping evil.

More recent treatments of just war have included the ideas that war must be the last resort after all other options have failed, and the means of prosecuting the war must be proportional to the offense of the nation deserving attack.

Those who are absolute pacifists usually disagree with the idea of a just war, asserting that all war is immoral and never "just." The presence of terrorists and the proliferation of weapons of mass destruction have caused many to rethink traditional beliefs about just war. In 2002, President George W. Bush of the United States declared that new circumstances make possible the use of *preemption*—the right to strike a nation or group first to avoid attack by the enemy nation or group in the future. This view has been rigorously debated.

39

THEODICY

BIG IDEA:

A theodicy is an attempt to defend the existence of God in light of the problem of evil in the world.

Some have argued that the presence of evil in the world is evidence against the existence of God. After all, how could an all-good and all-powerful God allow evil to exist? Not everyone, though, believes that the presence of evil in the world means that there is no God. Some have attempted to defend God in regard to the issue of evil in the world. This leads to the issue of "theodicy."

The term "theodicy" literally means "the justification of God." It is the attempt to reconcile God's positive attributes with the problem of evil. The term was allegedly popularized by **Gottfried Wilhelm Leibniz** in his *Essays in Theodicy*. The following are three major theodicies that have been offered:

1. Free Will Defense

Augustine promoted one form of theodicy called "the free will defense." This approach claims that God created human beings with the capacity to do both good and evil. Humans, however, chose to commit evil, and as a result, evil was introduced into the world. This theodicy claims that God was not wrong in granting humans free will since a world made of humans without free will would make the world of lesser quality. Important to this view is that humans are directly responsible for evil in the world—not God. This perspective is consistent with the traditional view that evil entered the world through the sin and fall of Adam and Eve.

2. Best Possible World

Leibniz offered a classic form of theodicy when he claimed that the world we have today, with evil, is a logical necessity. According to Leibniz, since God is perfect and all-good, he is obligated to create the best possible world since it is impossible for him to do otherwise. Thus, according to Leibniz, we can be confident that the world we have, which includes evil, is the best possible world. God's goodness is declared to be justified since God did what was best. Leibniz, like Augustine, blamed humans and not God for the evil in the world.

3. Irenaean Theodicy

The Irenaean theodicy is named after the second-century church father Irenaeus. This approach asserts that God made human beings with the need for "soul-making" or personal development. Since humans were made with the need to develop, God made the world with evil in it to give humans opportunities to grow spiritually. According to Irenaeus, this world is a "vale of tears" that prepares us for the next world to follow. This present world is not the best world, but it is the best path to the coming best world. Through participation in this imperfect world we become better prepared for the glorious world to come. A form of this approach has been promoted more recently by **John Hick**.

These three approaches are not the only theodicies. In recent decades, those known as process theologians have argued that God is all-good but not all-powerful. Thus, God is not able to totally stop all evil. Others, like Christian Scientists, have asserted that evil and sickness are largely illusions.

40

BOETHIUS

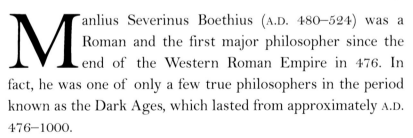

BIG IDEA:

The great ideas of philosophy can help you live a meaningful life.

anlius Severinus Boethius (A.D. 480–524) was a Roman and the first major philosopher since the end of the Western Roman Empire in 476. In fact, he was one of only a few true philosophers in the period known as the Dark Ages, which lasted from approximately A.D. 476–1000.

In his youth, Boethius wrote handbooks on mathematics and music. He also attempted a total translation of the works of **Plato** and **Aristotle**. This project was never finished, but Boethius's translations of Aristotle's logical works made these important writings available in the West for centuries to come.

An unorthodox thinker, Boethius was imprisoned for treason by the Gothic king Theodoric the Great around 523. Ironically, Boethius had hoped that Theodoric would become a model of the great "philosopher-king" that Plato wrote about. The specific charges against Boethius are unknown, and he was executed in 524.

In prison, Boethius wrote his most famous work, *The Consolations of Philosophy*. A dialog written in prose, this work describes a conversation Boethius had with the make believe Lady Philosophy who appears to him as the personification of wisdom. As Lady Philosophy visits Boethius in prison, she comforts him with advice from the great Greek philosophers of the past. She reminds him of the sufferings of **Socrates,** and she stresses the Stoic theme that a person's values are more important than circumstances. She also refers to Plato and Aristotle to show that wealth, power, and fame are not the keys to happiness.

Surprisingly, although Boethius was a Christian, his primary source of comfort was philosophy, not **Christianity**.

Boethius came along at an important time in history. At times he has been called the "Last of the Romans, first of the scholastics."

41

SCHOLASTICISM

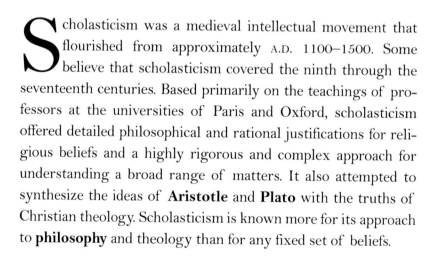

BIG IDEA:

Scholasticism offered detailed philosophical and rational justifications for theological topics.

Scholasticism was a medieval intellectual movement that flourished from approximately A.D. 1100–1500. Some believe that scholasticism covered the ninth through the seventeenth centuries. Based primarily on the teachings of professors at the universities of Paris and Oxford, scholasticism offered detailed philosophical and rational justifications for religious beliefs and a highly rigorous and complex approach for understanding a broad range of matters. It also attempted to synthesize the ideas of **Aristotle** and **Plato** with the truths of Christian theology. Scholasticism is known more for its approach to **philosophy** and theology than for any fixed set of beliefs.

Anselm of Canterbury is often viewed as the first great exponent of scholasticism. He originated the **ontological argument** for God's existence in which the concept of God itself is proof that God exists. **Thomas Aquinas** offered a natural theology in which truths about God, including God's existence, could be derived from the physical world. The embodiment of medieval scholasticism, Duns Scotus, offered complex discussions concerning being and **metaphysics**.

Because of their painstaking thoroughness in addressing abstract metaphysical and theological topics, the scholastic scholars (also known as the "schoolmen") have often been viewed as logical nitpickers. The irrelevant question, "How many angels can dance on the head of a pin?" became associated with the scholastics.

The humanists who came after the scholastics often viewed the scholastics as specializing in speculative nonsense that had no relevance. In fact, the derogatory term, "dunce," came from the name of the scholastic scholar, Duns Scotus. Some believe the title "scholasticism" was created by humanists who desired to discredit the scholastic scholars they despised.

Scholasticism largely disappeared at the end of the fifteenth century, but it has seen a modest revival within some pockets of Roman Catholicism.

42

ANSELM

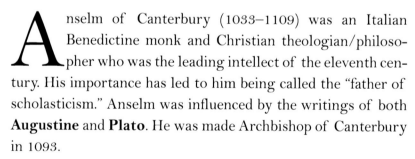

BIG IDEA:

God's existence can be proven through the ontological argument which asserts that the idea of God itself is proof that God exists.

nselm of Canterbury (1033–1109) was an Italian Benedictine monk and Christian theologian/philosopher who was the leading intellect of the eleventh century. His importance has led to him being called the "father of scholasticism." Anselm was influenced by the writings of both **Augustine** and **Plato**. He was made Archbishop of Canterbury in 1093.

Anselm was born in Aosta in what is now Italy. He stayed for thirty-seven years at the Benedictine monastery of Bec in Normandy from 1056 to 1093 when he was called to be archbishop in England. He is known for three things.

First, he attempted to show how reason was compatible with the Christian faith. Unlike other theologians of his era who argued exclusively from the Bible for their beliefs about reality, Anselm believed that reason could reveal certain truths about God and his works. Anselm is famous for his statement, *fides quarens intellectum,* which means "faith seeking understanding." Thus, for him, reason was not contrary to faith, but one needed to believe in order to best understand God and his world.

Second, Anselm is famous for formulating the **ontological argument** for God's existence. In his work *Proslogion,* Anselm asserted that the idea of God is proof that God exists. As he stated, "We believe that you [God] are a being than which nothing greater can be conceived." He also said, "Hence there is no doubt that there exists a being than which nothing greater can be conceived, and it exists both in the understanding and in reality." Anselm's ontological argument is unique in that it is an *a priori* argument—an argument of the mind and not of experience. Anselm's critic, Guanilo, chided Anselm, arguing that one could conceive of a perfect island, but that did not mean that such an island actually existed. Anselm countered by saying that it was possible to not conceive of a perfect island, but it was impossible to not conceive of God.

Third, Anselm is known for his arguments for the necessity of the Incarnation of Jesus Christ. In his *Cur Deus Homo* ("Why God Became Man"), he argued that Jesus' life and death were logical necessities. In doing so, he promoted what has become known as the "satisfaction theory" of the atonement. According to Anselm, God is like a king whose honor has been offended. Since God's honor and justice have been trampled, there must be an appropriate satisfaction for these offenses. This "satisfaction," though, must be equal to the offenses.

Because God is divine and humans are finite, there is no possible way that humans could pay the penalty needed to restore
God's honor. Jesus being divine, though, was able to pay the
satisfaction necessary. As both a representative of man and
God, Jesus satisfied God's honor and made a right relationship
with God possible.

43

RENAISSANCE

BIG IDEA:

The Renaissance signaled a "rebirth" of Greek and Roman culture and a turning away from the ideas of the Middle Ages.

The Renaissance was a cultural and literary movement that began in Italy (especially Rome and Florence) and spread to other areas of Europe including France, Germany, and England. The Renaissance Period lasted approximately from the late fourteenth century through the early sixteenth century. The term "renaissance" means "rebirth" and signified the rebirth of European culture after one thousand years of perceived cultural stagnation. In particular, the Renaissance involved a rediscovery of the previous Greek and Roman civilizations, which were viewed as being superior to European society during the Middle Ages.

The Renaissance is linked to **humanism** and its emphasis on human reason and achievement. The Renaissance stressed the importance of education. It also placed more emphasis on the physical world and less on the spiritual realm. This can be seen in the art of the period, which depicted more natural objects. The Renaissance Era also placed more emphasis on the individual. For example, during medieval times, most works of art depicted religious figures and events, and much of the art of the time was not autographed since doing so was considered an act of vanity. During the Renaissance, though, it was more common for artists to identify their own works.

Certain individuals, writings, and achievements are linked with the Renaissance Era. Galileo's scientific verification that the sun was the center of our solar system is viewed as the pivotal achievement of the Renaissance Period. **Niccolò Machiavelli's** work *The Prince* is often viewed as the classic Renaissance treatment of political philosophy because it discusses what rulers should do to remain in power. Erasmus, a Catholic theologian, is viewed by some as the preeminent scholar of the Renaissance. Other key figures of the Renaissance include the philosophers Nicholas Cusa (1401–1464), Giovanni Pico della Mirandola (1463–1494), and Giordano Bruno (1548–1600).

The Renaissance is often viewed as a bridge between the Medieval and Modern Eras, and its impact ushered in a period that became more man-centered and scientifically oriented.

44

HUMANISM

BIG IDEA:

The dignity and importance of man should be emphasized.

Humanism is a philosophy and attitude that stresses the importance and dignity of humans. Unlike some worldviews that stress the importance of God above all things, humanism focuses primarily on the importance, achievements, authority, and potential of people.

Humanism can be found at different points in history. In the fifth century B.C., the **Sophists** stressed social and moral questions. Humanism is often linked to the Renaissance Period of the fourteenth to early sixteenth centuries. During this time in some areas of Europe, there was a rediscovery of the art and literature of the ancient Greeks and Romans, which were viewed as superior to those of the Medieval Era. The

Renaissance Era also brought with it a renewed interest in the achievements and potential of man. Whereas in the Medieval Era most art and literature focused primarily on God and spiritual issues, art in the Renaissance Period focused more on man and nature.

While most in the Renaissance Era strongly believed in God, God's role in the universe was viewed as less immediate, and his participation in the world was seen as a general control and not so much as a moment-by-moment intervention. The Renaissance Era also saw an increased interest in education for the common people. Humanism was also furthered by the scientific discoveries of Copernicus, Galileo, and Newton.

In the nineteenth and twentieth centuries, humanism became more associated with **atheism** and **agnosticism**. The catalyst for this development was Charles Darwin's theory of **evolution**, which removed God from having an essential relationship with mankind. The secular humanism of today emphasizes the powers of reason, science, and education. It welcomes less focus on God and more emphasis on man to solve the problems facing humankind in the twenty-first century.

Not all who claim to be humanists today are secular humanists. Some believe in God and stress the importance and dignity of human beings.

45

ONTOLOGICAL ARGUMENT

BIG IDEA:

The idea of God is proof that God exists.

The ontological argument is an argument for God's existence based on the belief that the very idea of God is proof that God exists. The ontological argument is often stated like this: "God is the greatest being imaginable. One of the aspects of perfection or greatness is existence. Thus, God exists."

This argument for God's existence was developed by the twelfth-century theologian and philosopher **Anselm**. It was based on Anselm's declaration that God is "that which nothing greater can be conceived." Anselm's ontological argument is different from other major arguments for God's existence in that it is an *a priori* argument—an argument of the mind and not of experience.

The ontological argument can take different forms. **René Descartes**, for instance, promoted a form of this argument when he asserted that only God could place the idea of God within people. **Thomas Aquinas**, who promoted five arguments for God's existence, rejected the ontological argument.

The twentieth-century philosopher **Bertrand Russell** believed that the enterprise of **philosophy** had finally disproved ontological argument. The ontological argument, however, experienced a resurgence of support in the late twentieth century.

46

THOMAS AQUINAS

BIG IDEA:

Faith and reason are compatible.

homas from Aquino, or Saint Thomas Aquinas (1224–
1274), was an Italian theologian and philosopher who
is widely regarded as the greatest philosopher of the
Middle Ages.

His family was shocked when Thomas became a
Dominican monk. Viewing the Dominicans as a band of beg-
gars, his brothers kidnapped him and held him prisoner in the
family castle for a year. It is reported that his brothers tried to
lure him away from his calling with a prostitute. He chased her
away with a burning cross.

Aquinas eventually became a professor at the University
of Paris where he resided from 1252–1258. In his student days

he carried the nickname of "dumb ox" because he was quiet and perhaps overweight. Later he became more affectionately known as the "angelic doctor."

His most significant work was his *Summa Theologica*, which consists of over one and a half million words. The *Summa* was written for Christians and assumed the truths of the Bible. Another significant work of his was *Summa Contra Gentiles*, which was written for non-Christians and attempted to use arguments only from reason, not relying on the Bible.

Aquinas's contributions to **philosophy** are fourfold. First, Aquinas merged Christian theology with the teachings of the ancient Greek philosopher **Aristotle**. Although not the first person of his time to use Aristotle, Aquinas relied upon Aristotelian concepts when formulating his own views of philosophy and theology.

Second, Aquinas offered five proofs for God's existence, which upon review can be distilled into two main arguments— the **cosmological** and **teleological**. The cosmological argument asserts that all existing and contingent things like the earth rely upon some uncaused being for their existence. For Aquinas, the earth came into existence by the Christian God, who himself does not have a cause. (Aquinas's cosmological argument parallels Aristotle's concept of the "Prime Mover" that started all things in motion.) The teleological argument, which Aquinas also used, asserts that the incredible complexity in the universe points to an intelligent being that created it all. The universe, therefore, is not the result of blind chance.

Third, Aquinas argued that there was a close connection between faith and reason. For most of its history, the church viewed faith as superior to reason and saw no need to justify the truths of **Christianity** by the use of human reason. Aquinas, though, viewed faith and reason as working closely together. In fact, he believed reason could be used to justify many elements of the Christian faith. Unlike some theologians before and after him, Aquinas felt that Christianity did not need to fear reason. When used correctly, it affirmed some of what God had revealed in the Bible.

Fourth, Aquinas argued that nature reveals many truths about God. For example, studying nature could reveal to a person that God exists and that he is powerful. Thus, Aquinas believed we could learn about God by studying the world. Aquinas did not assert that everything we know about God comes from nature. There were some matters like the doctrine of the Trinity that could only be known through the Bible.

While Aquinas would be considered conservative by most standards today, many of his views were shocking to his contemporaries. He said that it was acceptable for a church to accept donations from a guild of prostitutes. He claimed that it was all right for married women to paint themselves (use cosmetics) to try to keep their husbands' affections. Aquinas held that the human embryo was only a plant at first, and then only a lower animal, and only later during pregnancy did it become human. For him, abortion was always wrong because one could never be sure at which stage an unborn child was at any given moment. Small wonder some of his writings were placed on a forbidden list in Paris during his lifetime!

St. Thomas Aquinas was canonized in 1323 and proclaimed a Doctor of the Church in 1567.

47

WILLIAM OF OCKHAM

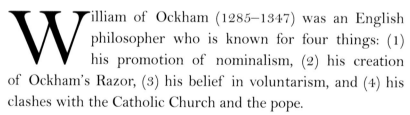

BIG IDEA:

*Needless hypotheses in arguments
need to be eliminated.*

Villiam of Ockham (1285–1347) was an English
philosopher who is known for four things: (1)
his promotion of nominalism, (2) his creation
of Ockham's Razor, (3) his belief in voluntarism, and (4) his
clashes with the Catholic Church and the pope.

First, William of Ockham was a nominalist because he
rejected the concept of **universals** and the belief that there are
independent metaphysical realities that objects in this world
partake of. (For example, some believe that redness is a universal in which particular objects such as red apples and fire
engines partake). Ockham, though, argued that universals were
unnecessary and needed to be eliminated. Since most medieval

philosophers of his era, including **Thomas Aquinas**, believed in universals, Ockham's stance against universalism and for nominalism was significant.

Second, William was concerned that the disciplines of **philosophy** and theology were loaded with far too many unnecessary hypotheses. In an effort to deal with the needless speculations of his day, Ockham created a figurative "razor" in which all needless hypotheses needed to be cut out. The doctrine of universals was one such concept that William believed needed to be sliced away from the study of philosophy.

Third, William promoted a form of voluntarism in which God is viewed as having absolute freedom to do whatever he wishes. According to William, God's acts are purely voluntary in that he does not have to act as he does. For example, God did not have to create the world or send his son, Jesus, to earth to die. Also, God could have chosen another way to save mankind if he so desired. William also asserted that since God is perfect and infinite, he is not bound by human reason, which is imperfect and finite. According to William, faith and reason cannot be reconciled. This approach led to the expansion of mysticism.

Fourth, William was known for his own life of poverty and the challenging of the luxurious lifestyle of the medieval church including that of Pope John XXII. A Catholic himself, William upset Pope John so much that the pontiff declared belief in apostolic poverty to be heretical. William also upset the church with his declaration that the Bible was the only infallible authority in matters of faith. This idea would be picked up later by Martin Luther and others associated with the Protestant Reformation. In spite of his troubles with the established church of his day, William was reconciled with the Roman Catholic Church before his death.

48

NICCOLÒ MACHIAVELLI

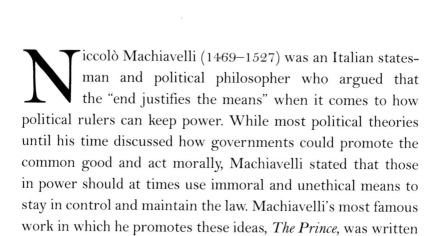

BIG IDEA:

*Rulers should use all means
necessary to stay in power.*

N iccolò Machiavelli (1469–1527) was an Italian states-
man and political philosopher who argued that
the "end justifies the means" when it comes to how
political rulers can keep power. While most political theories
until his time discussed how governments could promote the
common good and act morally, Machiavelli stated that those
in power should at times use immoral and unethical means to
stay in control and maintain the law. Machiavelli's most famous
work in which he promotes these ideas, *The Prince*, was written
in 1513 but was not published until after his death in 1532.

Machiavelli did not view himself as a philosopher, but he
saw himself as one who spoke frankly and practically about

keeping political power. According to Machiavelli, those born into power are more fortunate than those who must climb their way into authority since a man who rises to power must make enemies that will need to be eliminated.

For him, princes should use any means possible, including deceit, to maintain their territories. While arguing that a leader should do what he can to avoid being hated, he argued that death sentences would deter crime and that the people should often be dealt with severely and cruelly. But when they do so, their cruelty must be quick and severe since small retributions will often lead to revenge. Machiavelli also argued that it is better for a ruler to be feared than loved.

Machiavelli's views were controversial, and Pope Clement VIII condemned his teachings. To this day, rulers and leaders who act deceptively and unethically are often referred to as being "Machiavellian."

49

FRANCIS BACON

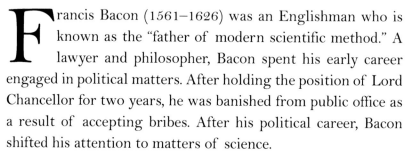

BIG IDEA:

The scientific method should be a regular part of man's endeavors.

Francis Bacon (1561–1626) was an Englishman who is known as the "father of modern scientific method." A lawyer and philosopher, Bacon spent his early career engaged in political matters. After holding the position of Lord Chancellor for two years, he was banished from public office as a result of accepting bribes. After his political career, Bacon shifted his attention to matters of science.

Bacon believed that people needed to use their powers of reason and observation to improve the situation of humankind. He reacted against the traditional medieval view that science was inferior to theology and asserted that men needed to understand and work with the laws of nature. From this belief came his famous statement, "Knowledge is power." Although not the greatest scientist himself, nor the first to undertake scientific pursuits, Bacon was a pioneer for science in that he actively called for and pursued a systematic scientific method in which the natural world was investigated in search of explanations.

In his work *Novum Organum*, Bacon promoted the concept of induction in which continual observation and experimentation should be conducted. He also asserted that prejudices and preconceived ideas, which he called "idols," should be abandoned. According to Bacon, there are four idols to be avoided. First, there are "idols of the tribe" in which people misread the laws of nature. Second, there are "idols of the cave" which refer to the subjective views of a person. Third, there are "idols of the marketplace" in which a loose use of language hinders the advance of reason. And fourth, there are "idols of theatre" in which tradition hinders the pursuit of truth.

Bacon viewed science as a social activity and desired to set up a college equipped with laboratories and botanical and zoological gardens. His death is almost as legendary as his life. He died of pneumonia as a result of trying to stuff a chicken with snow to prove that freezing temperatures could preserve meat.

50

DEISM

BIG IDEA:

Human reason is elevated above revelation from God, thus belief in God's existence is based on evidences from reason and nature and not on divine revelation.

D eism elevated human reason above divine revelation. It asserted that belief in God's existence is proven by reason and nature, not special revelation from the Bible. Closely associated with Deism is the idea that an intelligent and powerful being created the world, but this being is no longer involved with the world or intervenes in the affairs of people. With Deism, a being that could be called "God" made the world and set it in motion. But after creating the world and giving it the natural laws it needed to function, this being left the world, allowing it to function on its own. This God, who should not be understood as the personal God of **Christianity**, is like an absentee landlord, or a watchmaker who no longer has any interest in the watch he created.

The founder of Deism was Lord Herbert of Cherbury (1583–1648). Deism flourished in the seventeenth and eighteenth centuries and reached its zenith around the time of the American Revolution. This view was popular among European thinkers such as Voltaire as well as the Americans Thomas Jefferson and Benjamin Franklin.

In its early days, Deism was not as skeptical about traditional Christian views of God as it would become later. In fact, early on it was a revival of the natural theology of **Thomas Aquinas** in which nature teaches all people certain truths about God. Lord Herbert himself believed that natural theology supported Christian beliefs about God.

Eventually, though, Deism came to be viewed as an alternative view to Christianity. Matthew Tindal (1655–1733) published *Christianity as Old as the Creation*, which became known as the "Bible of Deism." In this work he argued a point that would become a central thesis of Deism—"reason is superior to revelation." Thus, if the truths of reason contradict the Christian message, a person should trust his or her own reason. Deists also eventually became the pioneers of radical Bible criticism, often denying the miraculous accounts in the Bible.

Joseph Butler (1692–1752) offered a refutation of Deism claiming that the truths of nature are consistent with the Bible. The radical skepticism of **David Hume** is also believed to have dealt a major death blow to Deism. As a movement, Deism did not survive into the nineteenth century.

Deists were initially attracted to the teleological argument for God's existence—namely that the great complexity in the world shows evidence of a designer. Antony Flew, a former leading defender of atheism, said that the complexity of the universe compelled him to believe in God. He acknowledged that his new view was similar to that of Deism.

51

RENÉ DESCARTES

BIG IDEA:

Human reason is the starting point for knowledge.

The famous philosopher René Descartes lived from 1596–1650. He was the most important philosopher of the seventeenth century and is one of the most significant philosophers in history. This "father of modern philosophy" was a Catholic who studied under the Jesuits. He spent most of his time in Protestant Holland. His most famous works were *Discourse on Method* and *Meditations on First Philosophy*.

Descartes believed he had a divine calling for coming up with philosophical ideas. On a winter day in 1619, while serving in the emperor's army, he conceived the idea of reforming human learning. That night he had three dreams that he regarded as prophetic signs for his divine vocation.

Descartes was dissatisfied with all previous studies of philosophy. He was frustrated that there was not one point of philosophy that could not be disputed. As a professional mathematician, Descartes wanted to root philosophy in the same certainty that mathematics possessed. Thus, he wanted to establish a starting point for philosophy that was as certain as mathematical truths. For him, once this certain starting point was established, then a system of philosophy could be constructed from this foundation.

As Descartes pursued the starting point of philosophy, he decided that he needed to rid himself of anything that could be doubted. Thus, he started with "radical doubt." For Descartes, even our five senses could not be trusted to give us a certain understanding of reality. In fact, Descartes said he had to be willing to doubt that his own body existed. "What if I think I am sitting in a chair by this stove, but in reality I'm only dreaming?" he said. "Maybe there is an evil demon playing a trick on my senses."

Finally, after removing all things that could be doubted, Descartes believed he found a starting point for philosophy—one thing that was beyond all dispute or doubt. What did he find?

Descartes asserted that the fact that he was thinking at all was proof that he existed. Even if he doubted his own existence, the very fact that he was involved with the activity of doubting must mean that he existed. Thus his famous declaration—*Cogito ergo sum*, which means "I think therefore I am." From this alleged undisputable finding, Descartes believed he could build a system of philosophy.

Descartes' theory had massive ramifications for philosophy. Before Descartes, God, church, pope, and the Bible were often viewed as starting points for knowledge and understanding reality. Although a strong Christian man himself, Descartes did not start with God to understand reality. Instead, he started with himself and his own reason. Descartes believed God helped people understand things clearly and did not intend to exclude God from philosophy, but he did not start with God to understand reality.

Thus, philosophers often say that Descartes shifted the focus in philosophy from God to the "subject" (human thinker). The starting point for knowledge now became the human thinker, not God. This was a significant departure from how philosophy was done in the past.

Descartes was talented in many areas. He was the founder of analytical geometry. He also researched the nature of the eye and light. His view that there was a distinction between the mind and the body became known as "Cartesian Dualism," a title named after him. Yet his most significant contribution was his attempt to establish a starting point for philosophy.

Descartes met an untimely death. Queen Christina of Sweden convinced Descartes to come to Sweden to be her personal tutor. A late riser, Descartes struggled with the 5:00 a.m. philosophy lessons the queen insisted upon. Descartes never adjusted, and many feel that this schedule and the cold Swedish winter led to his death in 1650.

52

RATIONALISM

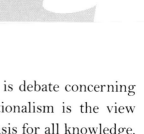

BIG IDEA:

Knowledge comes primarily through reason.

In the study of **epistemology** there is debate concerning where knowledge comes from. Rationalism is the view that reason is the primary or sole basis for all knowledge. Rationalism contrasts with **empiricism** and its assertion that all knowledge comes from a person's physical senses.

There are various forms of rationalism, but pure rationalism asserts that true and certain knowledge of the world can be found, and the way to find this knowledge is through mental processes. Those who believe in rationalism often assert that people are born with innate ideas that are not affected by our day-to-day experiences.

Rationalism was the view of several ancient Greek philosophers, especially **Plato**. The greatest rationalist of the Modern Era was **René Descartes**. Other important rationalists include **Gottfried Leibniz** and **Baruch Spinoza**.

53

SOLIPSISM

BIG IDEA:

*The only thing that exists
is one's self.*

What if only you existed and everything else was just an illusion? Solipsism is the view that the only thing a person can be absolutely sure of is that he or she exists. All other persons or objects do not exist independently and are merely projections of one's mind. The solipsist, therefore, views his or her mind as the only thing that exists in reality. All other persons and objects are reflections of his or her consciousness.

With solipsism, you may perceive things such as your house, car, newspaper, children, and spouse, but these things do not have a real, independent existence on their own. They are just conceptions in your mind, much like objects on a movie screen appear real but are really just reflections on a screen. Thus, the world that plays out before you is like images on your own private movie screen in which your mind is the projector.

The pre-Socratic Sophist philosopher Gorgias (c. 483–375 B.C.) is known as the first to promote solipsism. Forms of solipsism can be found in Eastern thought, particularly in Zen Buddhism and **Daoism**. It could be argued that solipsism has a philosophical base in the ideas of **René Descartes** and his *Cogito ergo sum*, which means "I think therefore I am." Using his approach of "radical doubt," Descartes argued that there was only one thing he could be absolutely sure of—the mere fact that he thinks means he must exist. Taken to an extreme, Descartes' view could be taken to mean that one can only be sure of one's own existence.

54

A PRIORI / A POSTERIORI

BIG IDEA:

A priori knowledge is knowledge that exists before experience; a posteriori knowledge is knowledge that comes after experience.

I s there knowledge that exists before experience? Or is knowledge something we acquire after experience? These questions relate directly to two categories of knowledge— *a priori* and *a posteriori.*

The term *a priori* comes from the Latin language and means "prior to experience." Thus, *a priori* knowledge is knowledge that exists before any experience with the physical world. The classic example of *a priori* truth is mathematics. The mathematical formulation "2+2=4" is said to be *a priori* because this truth comes from reflection alone and not from experience. Other examples of *a priori* knowledge would be the statements

"All men are created equal" or "It is self-evident that all men are entitled to life, liberty, and the pursuit of happiness."

A posteriori knowledge, on the other hand, is knowledge that comes after experience or observation of the physical world. The term *a posteriori* means "from what comes later" and, thus, refers to knowledge that comes as a result of physical experience. For example, the statement "Whatever goes up must come down" appears to be knowledge based on experience. We know from direct experience and from scientific observation that gravity works in such a way that objects that are thrown or launched into the air will eventually come back down to earth.

So which view of knowledge is correct? Great debate has existed throughout history concerning whether our knowledge is primarily *a priori* or *a posteriori*. **René Descartes** and **Gottfried Leibniz** were proponents of *a priori* knowledge. Descartes believed that knowledge of one's self was *a priori* since a person does not have to refer to past experience to contemplate one's existence. Others, like **John Locke** and **David Hume**, stressed that all of our knowledge comes from experience. In fact, Locke argued that our minds are a *tabula rasa* or "blank slate" at birth. Thus, it is only through experience of the world that we gain knowledge.

55

BIG IDEA:

People make a social contract with a sovereign in which they give up their rights in exchange for protection.

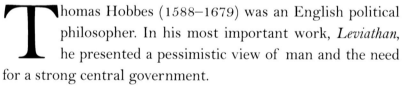

Thomas Hobbes (1588–1679) was an English political philosopher. In his most important work, *Leviathan*, he presented a pessimistic view of man and the need for a strong central government.

Hobbes asserted that humans begin life in a primitive "state of nature." In this state, people are equal in that they share relative equality in intelligence, strength, and experience. This equality, though, is not necessarily a good thing since it sets up situations in which struggles between equal but selfish and unprincipled humans take place. Apart from laws and social regulations, humans will continuously fight to get what they want. Hobbes called this the "war of every man against every man." Such a situation leads to a life that is "solitary, poor, nasty, brutish, and short."

Since chaos is the result of a society that does not have laws and regulations, Hobbes argued that a strong central government was necessary for the public good. Hobbes, thus, promoted a social contract theory in which men must make a contract with a sovereign ruler. With this contract the sovereign agrees to make and enforce laws that will keep the peace. The people, on the other hand, give up some of their liberties and agree to obey the laws of the sovereign, who himself is not subject to civil law. The people are under obligation to obey the sovereign unless he becomes unable to protect them. Hobbes recognized three forms of government—monarchy, aristocracy, and democracy. He believed that monarchy was the most effective form for promoting peace.

As for his views on reality, Hobbes was a materialist. Everything, including humans, is a set of particles moving in accordance with the laws of nature. He was also an empiricist who acknowledged the importance of mathematics. For Hobbes, religion was invented by men because of their ignorance and fears. In addition, he asserted that concepts like good, evil, and justice are solely dependent on what a sovereign ruler declares them to be.

56

PASCAL'S WAGER

BIG IDEA:

It is preferable to wager in favor of God's existence than to bet on the opposite idea that God does not exist.

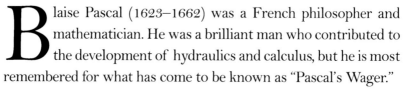

laise Pascal (1623–1662) was a French philosopher and mathematician. He was a brilliant man who contributed to the development of hydraulics and calculus, but he is most remembered for what has come to be known as "Pascal's Wager."

Pascal, who had developed the mathematics of probability in relation to gambling activities such as dice, applied the idea of a "wager" to belief in the existence of God. According to Pascal, it was better for a person to wager in favor of God's existence than to bet on the opposite idea that God did not exist. Why? The answer is related to the consequences of each option.

If a person wagers on God's existence and it ends up being true that God does indeed exist, then that person will inherit eternal life. If the end result is that God does not exist, though, then the believer loses little. He merely ceases to exist. On the other hand, if a person chooses to not believe in God and God does exist, then that person will suffer the horrible consequences of eternal punishment in hell. For Pascal, then, the choice was clear. If you are undecided as to whether to believe in God or not, the smart thing to do is to wager on God's existence.

Pascal's Wager differs from other traditional arguments for God's existence in that it does not attempt to show that God exists. Rather, it focuses on why people should believe in God's existence. Pascal himself did not emphasize the use of reason for religious purposes. For him, faith in God was a gift and not the result of traditional cause and effect arguments for God's existence.

Some have offered criticisms of Pascal's Wager. For example, some say that believing in God because of fear that God might exist is not really true belief. Plus, others have asserted that Pascal assumes the Christian God as the correct object of belief. But what about other religions that have different gods? It appears that one could choose to believe in a god of one religion but still be damned for choosing the wrong god.

57

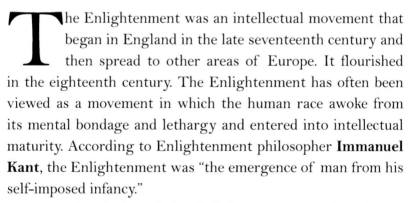

ENLIGHTENMENT

BIG IDEA:

Human reason alone is the highest source of knowledge.

The Enlightenment was an intellectual movement that began in England in the late seventeenth century and then spread to other areas of Europe. It flourished in the eighteenth century. The Enlightenment has often been viewed as a movement in which the human race awoke from its mental bondage and lethargy and entered into intellectual maturity. According to Enlightenment philosopher **Immanuel Kant**, the Enlightenment was "the emergence of man from his self-imposed infancy."

The foundation of the Enlightenment was the primacy of human reason. In contrast to earlier eras in which popes, priests, traditions, and holy books were the authorities, the

Enlightenment stressed that human reason was the highest authority. In fact, a motto of the Enlightenment could be, "Reason over revelation." The Enlightenment also stressed the overall goodness of people. While acknowledging that people could act wickedly, old views concerning original sin and the depravity of man were replaced with an optimistic perspective concerning man's nature. Man could overcome evil by his own efforts through reason and education.

Also characteristic of this new "Age of Reason" was an optimism regarding the betterment of society. Reason, education, science, and technology were believed to be ushering in an era of "technological messianism" in which many of the world's problems would be solved and a golden era of ideal living conditions would occur. The Enlightenment also stressed the equality of all persons, believing that all people were endowed with natural rights. It rejected the traditional view of the "divine right of kings" in which kings were viewed as possessing their authority directly from God.

The Enlightenment brought serious challenges to traditional religion, especially **Christianity**. Miracles and supernatural accounts were often rejected since they were viewed as being incompatible with reason. The Enlightenment also spawned the discipline of biblical criticism, which became popular in the major universities of Europe. As a result, the Bible was subjected to sustained and withering criticisms. For instance, traditional authorships of Bible books were often rejected, and anything supernatural in the Bible was dismissed or reinterpreted.

While some Enlightenment thinkers still embraced traditional Christianity, the Enlightenment spawned a good share of atheists, agnostics, and Deists. **David Hume** left no room for God or the miraculous. Immanuel Kant, while himself a believer in God, laid the philosophical basis for **agnosticism** by arguing that the noumenal (nonmaterial) realm was totally unknowable by reason. Thus, nothing about God, the soul, or the afterlife could be known through reason.

Deists like Thomas Jefferson believed that the existence of a creator was compatible with reason, but this creator was not the Christian God and certainly not a being that cared about or interacted with humans. It was this stinging rejection and dismantling of traditional Christianity that led to the birth of liberal Christianity. The founder of liberal Christianity, **Friedrich Schleiermacher**, tried to adjust Christianity to make it more palatable to modern man. In so doing, he rejected traditional Christian beliefs such as the virgin birth and the deity of Jesus Christ.

The beginnings of the Enlightenment are often linked with the views of **John Locke** and the English Deists. This movement eventually spread to France in the eighteenth century and was developed in the writings of Voltaire and Denis Diderot. Eventually, the Enlightenment reached Germany and other parts of Europe.

It is difficult to date precisely when the Enlightenment Era ended, although some point to the French Revolution (1789–1799) as the end of this movement. In today's postmodern world several key assumptions of the Enlightenment have been rejected, including high confidence in reason and the belief that reality makes sense and can be truly understood.

58

BARUCH SPINOZA

BIG IDEA:

There is only one substance in the world—God or nature.

Baruch Spinoza (1632–1677) was a Dutch philosopher who was also a lens grinder by trade. An independent and solitary thinker, Spinoza refused academic appointments and decided not to teach at the University of Heidelberg because he did not want to be restricted by the established ideas of any academic institution.

Spinoza is most known for his promotion of monism, the idea that there is only one single substance in the world—God or nature (*Deus sive natura*). This idea was contrary to the concept of **dualism** and its idea that reality was made of two substances—mind and matter. For Spinoza, mind and matter were two modes of the single substance—God/nature. Thus, there is no distinction between mind and matter because both are different manifestations of God/nature.

With Spinoza's monism, any statement about any object is a statement about God or nature. This view has often been linked with **pantheism**—the belief that God is nature and nature is God. Spinoza rejected belief in the immortality of the soul.

Educated as an Orthodox Jew, Spinoza became unpopular with both Jews and Christians because of his unorthodox beliefs. For example, Spinoza argued for a late dating of the Old Testament books and denied the miracles of the Bible. He was considered by some to be a closet atheist. In 1656, he was excommunicated from his Jewish community and synagogue in Amsterdam because of his nontraditional views.

In 1677, Spinoza died from glass dust inhalation. After his death, his works were largely ignored and viewed as the dangerous works of a closet atheist. Although his ideas were difficult to understand, they were eventually discovered by Gotthold Lessing. The writings of Spinoza eventually had a significant impact on the beliefs of **Georg Hegel**.

59

PANTHEISM

BIG IDEA:

*God is everything and
everything is God.*

P antheism is the view that identifies God with the world
and everything in the world. Or put another way—
"God is everything and everything is God." The term
"pantheism" comes from two Greek terms—*pan*, which means
"all," and *theos*, which means "God." Thus, pantheism literally means "all is God." With pantheism, there is a unity to all
things, and any statement about any object is really a statement
about God. The term was first coined by John Toland in the
early eighteenth century to identify philosophical systems that
identified God with the world.

Important to pantheism is the view that there is no sepa-
ration between God and the universe. This position is contrary

to what is taught in the monotheistic religions of Judaism, **Christianity**, and Islam. These religions teach that God is transcendent, which means that God is separate from and independent of the time-space universe. Pantheism is more in line with the concept of immanence in which God is intrinsically a part of the universe.

Various religions and philosophers throughout history have held pantheistic beliefs. Some Native American religions and Hinduism contain pantheistic elements. So also do pagan and nature religions such as Wicca. The most famous philosophical promoter of pantheism was **Baruch Spinoza**. Spinoza asserted that there is only one substance in the universe and this substance is divine. He is famous for declaring—"*Deus sive natura*," which means "God or nature."

Some evaluators of pantheism have identified it as a mediating position between traditional theism and **atheism**. Others have seen it as a form of atheism since it denies the presence of a personal God.

60

JOHN LOCKE

BIG IDEA:

Sovereignty and power belong to the people and not the government.

John Locke (1632–1704) was an English philosopher who is known for three main contributions: (1) founding the school of **empiricism**, (2) promoting democratic political theories, and (3) espousing the theory of primary and secondary qualities.

In regard to empiricism, Locke argued that the foundation for knowledge comes from experience, not intuitive reasoning or innate ideas. Thus, experience imprints knowledge. According to Locke, the mind of a person at birth is a *tabula rasa*—a "blank slate." He promoted empiricism in his work *Essay Concerning Human Understanding*.

In his work *Two Treatises of Government*, Locke espoused a political theory that denied the theory of "divine right of kings" and its view that the king's authority comes directly from God and not the people. For Locke, sovereignty belongs to the people, not the government. He also believed that a government should have a system of checks and balances. Locke argued that all people have natural rights in regard to life, liberty, and property. The purpose of government is to protect these rights. If the state does not do this, the people can remove or alter it. Thus, rebellion can be justified under certain conditions. Although he died seventy years before the American Revolution, many of his political ideas were adopted into the U.S. Constitution.

Locke was also known for his views on qualities. He asserted that objects have two qualities—primary and secondary. Primary qualities are the qualities of a thing that exist independently of a perceiver. For example, an object's shape and size are fixed whether a perceiver is viewing the object or not. On the other hand, secondary qualities are the qualities of a thing that depend for their existence on a perceiver. Examples include an object's sound and taste, which appear to be relative to a perceiver.

61

BIG IDEA:

*The world we live in is the
best of all possible worlds.*

Gottfried Wilhelm Leibniz (1646–1716) was a rationalist philosopher who was born in what is now Germany.
Brilliant in many areas, he became famous for: (1) his
view of monads and (2) his promotion of a unique **theodicy**.

Leibniz, the son of a professor of moral philosophy, was
rightly considered a genius by his contemporaries since he was
an expert in many different fields. As an engineer, he worked
on clocks, mining machines, and calculating instruments. As a
librarian, he invented the idea of cataloguing books. As a physi-
cist, he furthered the study of mechanics and the theory of
momentum. As a mathematician, Leibniz independently came
up with calculus around the same time as Isaac Newton. In

addition, Leibniz developed principles of logic and formulated the Law of Non-Contradiction. He is also known for developing the Principle of Sufficient Reason—the view that all things happen for a reason; nothing is just a matter of random chance.

Leibniz is famous for his complicated view of monads. According to Leibniz, there are metaphysical realities called monads. These immaterial monads are the only substances that actually exist. Matter, therefore, does not exist but is only the appearance of monads. The study of the physical world, therefore, is really a study of appearances (or the phenomenal realm). These monads are "windowless" in that they do not have any causal relationships with each other. God is the one who creates these monads. He programs each monad with various perceptions. All monads together express the universe that we have.

Leibniz also pioneered the concept of "**theodicy**," which literally means "justification of God." He coined this term in his work *Essays in Theodicy* as he defended God in light of the problem of evil. According to Leibniz, the world we have, with evil in it, is the best of all possible worlds. Since God is perfect and good, he had to create the best world from a realm of other possible worlds. This does not mean, though, that God is the author of evil, according to Leibniz. Evil results from the misuse of human freedom.

62

GEORGE BERKELEY

BIG IDEA:

*The only things that exist
are minds and ideas in
the mind.*

George Berkeley (1685–1753) was an Irish philosopher and bishop in the Anglican Church. He is known as the founder of subjective idealism—the view that the external world does not exist independently of a human or divine mind. Thus, the only things that exist are minds and ideas in the mind. He also believed in immaterialism—the theory that there is no matter in the universe.

So what are objects like trees and other things that we think we see, according to Berkeley? They are collections of ideas or sensations that exist only if perceived. Thus, all experiences are illusions. Remember the question: "If a tree falls in a forest and no one sees it, did it really happen?" According to

Berkeley, neither the tree nor the forest would exist if not perceived by some mind.

Berkeley is famous for the statement: *Esse est percipi* – "to be is to be perceived." The prolific English writer, Samuel Johnson, responded to Berkeley's **idealism** by kicking a stone. "I refute him thus," said Johnson. According to Berkeley, the presence of God, who always perceives everything, gives a sense of permanence to matters. Since God perceives things, they continually are in a sense of "being."

Berkeley wrote his important philosophical books from 1709 to 1713 while he was still in his twenties. He became a bishop in 1734. Berkeley had a great effect on higher education while in America. He assisted in the development of what came to be Yale and Columbia universities, and he tried to establish a school for Native Americans. The University of California, Berkeley, is named after him.

63

IDEALISM

BIG IDEA:

*The external world does not
exist apart from the mind.*

I dealism is a metaphysical theory about the nature of reality that asserts that the external world does not exist independently of the human mind. Thus, only ideas exist. In contrast to materialism, which views matter and energy as the only realities, idealism asserts that reality exists in our minds and not in the external world.

Plato's theory of forms is often viewed as a form of idealism. The first true idealist philosopher, however, was **George Berkeley**, who claimed that all objects are collections of ideas or sensations. Thus, something only exists if it is being perceived by the mind. His famous statement in this regard was *Esse est percipi* – "to be is to be perceived." Berkeley's position naturally coincided with "immaterialism"—the view that there is no matter in the universe.

Immanuel Kant held to a form of idealism called "transcendental idealism." This perspective asserts that knowledge of the world is dependent on the conceptual processes of the human mind. Humans, thus, cannot know things as they are in themselves.

Another form of idealism is "absolute idealism." This view holds that there is a universal self-consciousness or notion that makes reality what it is. The most famous absolute idealist was **Georg Hegel** who claimed that all reality is shaped by *Geist*, which means "Spirit" or "Mind."

There are several forms of idealism, but all idealists agree that there is no access to reality apart from the mind and what the mind provides.

64

FEMINISM

BIG IDEA:

Women need to throw off oppression from a male-dominated society and pursue equal treatment in all areas of life.

Feminism is a movement that pays special attention to the rights and position of women in society, calling on equal treatment for women in all areas of life. Although there are many forms of feminism, feminism has traditionally tried to remedy pervasive discrimination and mistreatment of the female gender. The word "feminism" was coined by the socialist philosopher Charles Fourier, and was first used in English in the 1890s.

Feminists point out that for most of human history women have been treated as subordinate and inferior to men. They claim this is evidenced in the fact that the great leaders, rulers, and philosophers throughout history have been over-whelmingly male. Plus, feminists often believe that societies and religions have perpetuated the belief that a woman's place in society is mainly that of raising a family and helping her husband. According to some feminists, this suppression of women and women's rights has been engrained into societies for so long that most women passively accept subordination to men as part of life. That is why they believe the feminist movement is necessary.

Modern feminism began to take shape in the eighteenth century. Mary Wollstonecraft (1759–1797) is often viewed as the founder of the modern feminist movement. In her book *A Vindication of the Rights of Women,* Wollstonecraft called for equal educational opportunities for women. In 1851, the feminists Elizabeth Cady Stanton and Susan B. Anthony joined together in a fifty-year fight for equal rights for women in the social and civil realms.

Feminists tasted victory in the early part of the twentieth century when women were granted the right to vote. After this triumph, the focus of the feminist movement shifted to equal social and economic positions for women. Important feminists of the twentieth century include **Simone de Beauvoir**, Betty Friedan, and Gloria Steinem. In addition to pushing for equal rights and treatment for women in all areas, the feminist movement of today is most noted for its promotion and defense of abortion rights. Many feminists today also decry what they believe to be the sexual objectification of women in the media and entertainment industries.

65

TELEOLOGICAL ARGUMENT

BIG IDEA:

The appearance of design and complexity in the universe argues for a God that created and designed it.

The teleological argument (or the "argument from design") is an argument for God's existence based on the belief that the appearance of design and complexity in the universe argue for a creator. The teleological argument goes like this: "The universe and its contents evidence great complexity. Since great complexities such as the human body and the movements in our solar system cannot happen by random chance, some powerful and intelligent being must have created the universe. This divine architect is God."

One modern proponent of the teleological argument was William Paley (1743–1805), who used the analogy of a watch to promote the view that God created the world. According to Paley, just as a watch implies the existence of a watch-maker, the design of the universe implies the existence of a universe-maker.

Some believe that **David Hume** seriously damaged the validity of the teleological argument when he challenged traditional views concerning cause and effect. There have been three traditional responses to the teleological argument. First, some say the teleological argument is guilty of a "weak analogy" because it assumes a significant resemblance between natural objects (e.g., rocks, trees) and objects we know have been designed (e.g., watches, skyscrapers). Second, some say that the theories of the big bang and evolution better explain the complexities in the universe. Third, some say that even if the teleological argument is true, it does not prove the existence of the Christian God.

The teleological argument continues to be widely held today and might be the most influential of the traditional arguments for God's existence. The famous English philosopher, Antony Flew (1923–2010), rejected his former belief in atheism based largely on the teleological argument. He said, "The argument to Intelligent Design is enormously stronger than it was when I first met it." Thus, Flew adopted a form of deism comparable to that of another famous deist—Thomas Jefferson.

66

DAVID HUME

BIG IDEA:

Experience and reason cannot show causal connections between objects.

Can we know with certainty that one thing causes another? For instance, do you know for certain that the purple spot on your white carpet was caused from the grape juice that was spilled two seconds earlier? Does past observation tell us that the sun will rise in the east tomorrow or that trees will lose their leaves in the fall? Not necessarily so, according to David Hume.

David Hume (1711–1776) was a famous Scottish philosopher who was known for his skeptical views regarding the certainty of knowledge. Hume challenged traditional views of cause and effect and argued that reason and experience cannot show a certain connection between objects. Thus, conclusions based on past experience and observations are not certain. One cannot know for sure that a tree will lose its leaves this autumn. Also, past experience and reason do not guarantee that the sun will rise tomorrow. Hume used the game of billiards to illustrate his view of cause and effect. According to Hume, one may assume that the stick hits the white ball, which in turn hits the red ball, but one cannot know for sure that there is a causal connection between the white and red balls.

Hume was also famous for his skepticism in regard to **metaphysics** and religion. He rejected traditional religion, believing that it was a cover for prejudice and dogmatism. He believed that all religious sentiment comes from two emotions—hope and fear. Hume also asserted that the existence of God cannot be proven by arguments from cause and effect. He attacked the **ontological**, **cosmological**, and **teleological** proofs for God's existence and did not accept the argument from miracles for the existence of God. According to Hume, the report of a miracle was more likely to be false than true because miracles simply do not happen.

Along with **John Locke** and **George Berkeley**, Hume is often identified with the British Empiricist School. Some believe his views took him beyond empiricism to skepticism. Hume had a major impact on the philosopher **Immanuel Kant**, who declared that Hume had awoken him from his "dogmatic slumbers." Hume's famous works include *An Enquiry concerning Human Understanding, A Treatise of Human Nature,* and *An Enquiry concerning the Principles of Morals.* He also wrote *Dialogues concerning Natural Religion.*

Hume—one of the most learned men of his day—tried to obtain professorships in Scotland but was turned down because his views appeared to be too close to atheism. Hume's skepticism in regard to causation and religion is still influential today. He died of bowel cancer in 1776.

67

EMPIRICISM

BIG IDEA:

All knowledge comes only from sense experience.

mpiricism is the view that all knowledge comes from sense experience. It is the opposite of **rationalism**, which claims that knowledge stems from innate ideas in the mind. Thus, with empiricism the five senses are the basis for knowledge. Empiricism is often viewed as being at the heart of the modern scientific method since it stresses observation of the physical world.

Empiricist ideas can be traced to the ancient Greeks. In contrast to **Plato**, who stressed "forms" and "ideas" as the true realities in another dimension, **Aristotle** stressed earthly realities as being at the heart of reality.

Empiricism, though, officially developed in the seventeenth and eighteenth centuries with the teachings of **John Locke, George Berkeley**, and **David Hume**. Locke, in particular, is known for pioneering the empiricist school. He argued that the mind of a person at birth is a *tabula rasa*, which refers to a "blank slate."

These three empiricists—Locke, Berkeley, and Hume—are often known as comprising the British Empiricist School. This school reacted against the rationalism of the influential rationalist **René Descartes**.

68

JEAN JACQUES ROUSSEAU

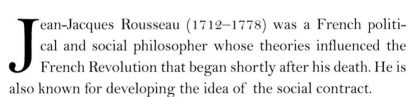

BIG IDEA:

*People are by nature good but
become corrupted by society.*

Jean-Jacques Rousseau (1712–1778) was a French political and social philosopher whose theories influenced the French Revolution that began shortly after his death. He is also known for developing the idea of the social contract.

Rousseau's mother died at his birth. He had almost no family upbringing, and he had no formal education. In his work *Social Contract* (1762), Rousseau promoted a high view of human nature that was more optimistic than those of his contemporaries, especially **Thomas Hobbes**.

Rousseau promoted a state-of-nature scenario in which all people are viewed as autonomous individuals whose primary desire is self-preservation. Since people are autonomous, the concept of society goes against their very nature. Rousseau's famous statement was, "Man is born free, and everywhere he is in chains." The "chains" refer to restricting societal relationships such as marriage, family, church, and the workplace. According to Rousseau, society corrupts the inherent goodness of people. Society also chokes the freedom that people have in their state of nature.

Rousseau denied that the strong have the right to rule over the weak. Government should only exist as long as ultimate sovereignty stays with the people. Thus, the state can be overthrown if it fails to adequately express the general will of the people.

When he first arrived in Paris, Rousseau strived to be a musical theorist and composer. He was also an avid writer on botany. He became a writing companion of Voltaire and a personal friend of Diderot, who eventually invited him to write articles on music and political economy for the new French encyclopedia.

After the publication of his works *Social Contract* and *Emile*, Rousseau fled Paris to avoid persecution since his views were viewed as a threat to traditional religion.

69

IMMANUEL KANT

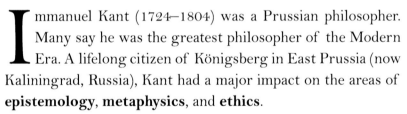

BIG IDEA:

There is a significant distinction between how things appear and what they actually are.

Immanuel Kant (1724–1804) was a Prussian philosopher. Many say he was the greatest philosopher of the Modern Era. A lifelong citizen of Königsberg in East Prussia (now Kaliningrad, Russia), Kant had a major impact on the areas of **epistemology**, **metaphysics**, and **ethics**.

Kant both studied and taught at the University of Königsberg. As a professor, he was well-liked by his students. He was only 5 feet tall. A punctual man, it is said that the people of Königsberg set their watches according to his daily walk schedule.

Kant says the writings of **David Hume** awoke him from his "dogmatic slumbers." In regard to **epistemology** (the study of knowledge), Kant was revolutionary in that he synthesized two competing schools of thought—**rationalism** (knowledge comes from innate ideas in the mind) and **empiricism** (knowledge comes only from experience).

In agreement with the empiricists, Kant held that all our knowledge *comes* from experience, but he also claimed that all our knowledge does not *arise* out of experience. Unlike the empiricists, Kant claimed that our minds are not passive; instead, our minds actively sort, organize, and synthesize sense data that comes to us through our five senses. Thus, our minds are programmed to interpret the physical data we experience.

Also important to Kant's philosophy was his distinction between phenomena and noumena. For Kant, phenomena are things as they appear to us. Noumena, on the other hand, are things as they really are in themselves. Thus, there is a difference between things as they really are and how people perceive these things. According to Kant, each person views things in the world through his or her own Forms of Intuition and Categories of Understanding. As a result, no person is able to understand objects perfectly. Even in the material realm, no one is able to fully understand things as they actually are.

Kant's philosophy was even more skeptical in regard to metaphysical issues like God, the soul, and freedom. According to Kant, these issues are beyond the limits of reason. Thus, the human mind cannot obtain any rational knowledge of anything beyond the physical world.

Kant's theory would have an important influence on the **philosophy of religion** since he asserted that concepts like God and the soul could not be known through reason. His theories have led some to claim that he is the "father of **agnosticism**." Interestingly, Kant did believe in God and originated a form of the moral-law argument for God's existence. He is famous for saying "Two things fill the mind with ever new and increasing admiration and awe . . . The starry heavens above me and the moral law within me."

Kant also impacted the area of **ethics**. For him, "motive" is the most important factor in determining what is ethical. More specifically, Kant argued that a moral action is one that is performed out of a "sense of duty." Thus, for Kant, a moral action is not based upon feelings or pity. Nor is it based on the possibility of reward. Instead, a moral action is one based on a sense of "This is what I ought to do." Another important aspect of Kant's ethical system is his **categorical imperative**, which declares: "Act on a maxim [principle] that you would rationally want to apply to everybody." Thus, for Kant, a person should act in such a way that, if possible, his or her action would become the universal law by which everyone else in the world should act under similar circumstances.

Kant wrote several significant works including his *Critique of Pure Reason*. Ironically, Kant never left Königsberg for any significant length of time, but his philosophy had a worldwide impact. In his later years, Kant began to lose his memory, something that frustrated him greatly. He died in 1804 at the age of 80.

70

KANTIAN ETHICS

BIG IDEA:

Motive is the most important factor in ethics.

Kantian ethics is based upon the teachings of the philosopher **Immanuel Kant** (1724–1804). According to Kant, the concept of "motive" is the most important factor in determining what is ethical. More specifically, Kant argued that a moral action is one that is performed out of a "sense of duty."

For Kant, a moral action is not based upon feelings or pity. Nor is it based on the possibility of reward. Instead, a moral action is one based on a sense of "This is what I ought to do." To use an example, helping an old lady across the street because you feel pity for her is *not* a moral act. Likewise, helping an old lady because your coworker will think highly of you is not a moral act. However, helping an old lady because you have a sense of duty to help the elderly is moral.

Because motive is the most important factor in Kantian ethics, it is possible for an action to have negative consequences while still being a moral act. For example, if acting out of a sense of duty you attempt to save a drowning child, but in the process you accidentally drown the child, your action could still be considered a moral one.

Kantian ethics has been criticized on several points. First, some say Kant's approach gives little aid for complex situations. For example, what if there are conflicts of duty? Suppose you decide that two duties are (1) telling the truth and (2) protecting your friends. But what if a madman with an axe asks you where your best friend is so he could murder her? Do you tell the truth and thus lead the murderer to your friend? Or do you lie and save your friend's life? Interestingly, Kant believed telling a lie was always wrong even if a vicious murderer asked him where his friend was.

71

CATEGORICAL IMPERATIVE

BIG IDEA:

Act in such a way that, if possible, what you do should automatically become a universal law that everyone should follow in similar circumstances.

In the realm of **ethics, Immanuel Kant** promoted what has become known as the "categorical imperative." The categorical imperative is a method for rationally and objectively determining which action a person should take when faced with an ethical situation. According to Kant, the categorical imperative is, "Act on a maxim [principle] that you would rationally want to apply to everybody." In other words, act in such a way that, if possible, your action would become a universal law for everyone facing a similar situation. With this approach, for an action to be moral the underlying principle behind it must be *universal*—it should hold true for everyone in similar situations.

Thus, the key question you must ask yourself when facing a situation is this: "Would I want everyone to do this?"

For example, suppose you are about to get in line at the grocery store and you contemplate cutting into that line without permission. Applying the categorical imperative, you should ask yourself if your potential response is rational and is what everyone else should do in the same circumstance. Would you want everyone else in the world to cut into lines while waiting at a store? Applying the categorical imperative, if everyone decided to cut into lines at stores, there would be no lines since excessive cutting into lines would lead to chaos and no more lines at stores and perhaps no more grocery stores at all. Based on this scenario, cutting into a line at a store is irrational and should be avoided.

Kant himself used the example of depression and suicide. Suppose you are deeply depressed and you contemplate suicide as being in your self-interest. Should you commit suicide? No, according to Kant. Committing suicide is inconsistent with pursuing your self-interest. Plus, if everyone committed suicide because they were depressed, then the human race would suffer irreversible harm and even extinction. Thus, committing suicide when depressed is an unreasonable action and should be avoided.

In creating the categorical imperative, Kant tried to create a logical, reasonable, and non-emotional approach to ethics. Some have criticized the categorical imperative saying that it is too simplistic in complex situations. Others have said that it wrongly rules out emotions and feelings in the determination of what is ethical.

72

AGNOSTICISM

BIG IDEA:

God is unknowable.

C an God be known through human reason? Is there enough evidence to conclude that God exists? In regard to the issue of God, agnosticism is the view that God's existence cannot be known. The term comes from the Greek language and can be translated literally into English as "no knowledge." In the realm of **metaphysics** (the study of reality), then, agnosticism is the view that there is "no knowledge" concerning God.

Agnosticism can take two forms. The first is that knowledge of God is not possible through reason. **Immanuel Kant** took this view when he argued that matters outside of the physical realm, like God and the soul, were unknowable to human reason.

The second form of agnosticism asserts that God's existence is simply not known. A person espousing this second form of agnosticism would say, "I just don't know if there is a God or not."

Agnosticism should not be confused with **atheism**—the view that God does not exist. The word "agnostic" was first used by T. H. Huxley in 1869. Huxley was a British biologist who agreed with Charles Darwin's theory of evolution. With intellectual curiosity, Huxley sought to discover whether he was an atheist, theist, pantheist, materialist, or idealist. Not convinced about the certainty of any of these options, Huxley sought a term that described his uncertainty. "So I took thought, and invented what I conceived to be the appropriate title of 'agnostic,'" said Huxley. "To my great satisfaction the term took."

73

FRIEDRICH SCHLEIERMACHER

BIG IDEA:

Christianity must be reconstructed in light of the Enlightenment's critique of traditional Christianity.

F riedrich Schleiermacher (1768–1834) was a German theologian and philosopher who became known as the founder of modern Protestant Liberalism and modern hermeneutics. He is also known as the theologian of **Romanticism**.

In the wake of the **Enlightenment**, traditional **Christianity** had been savaged by skeptical critiques of the Bible and anything supernatural. Schleiermacher, though, attempted to reconstruct Christianity in a way that was more acceptable to the modern mind. While clinging to the title "Christian," Schleiermacher denied essential Christian truths such as the

Fall of Man, the inspiration of the Bible, the Trinity, the deity of Jesus, and the second coming of Jesus.

Schleiermacher's key concept was "feeling," or "feeling of absolute dependence." He stressed religious experience over cognitive belief in some divine being that was "out there." Schleiermacher's key contribution to **philosophy** is that he tried to alter Christianity in light of the philosophical ideas of the Enlightenment and place "feeling" over cognitive revelation. Modern liberalism was spawned from his idea that religious experience trumps traditional doctrines.

Schleiermacher also constructed a detailed theory of interpretation (or hermeneutics). He argued for "authorial intent" in which communication is a direct encounter between reader and author. By trying to understand the world of the author, the reader can tap into the intent of the author.

Finally, Schleiermacher was important to Romanticism in that he stressed the subjective and experiential elements of Christianity. This viewpoint is consistent with Romanticism's emphasis on the subjective and personal experiences of man.

Schleiermacher became a clergyman in 1796 and played a prominent role in the union of the Lutheran and Reformed churches in Prussia in 1817.

74

GEORG W. F. HEGEL

BIG IDEA:

All reality is the outworking of "Spirit."

Georg Wilhelm Friedrich Hegel (1770–1831) was a German philosopher who boldly set forth a philosophical system that allegedly comprehended and explained the entire course of history. A university lecturer and a professor of philosophy, Hegel wrote in a manner that was incomprehensible to many. In fact, some have asserted that Hegel is perhaps the most difficult philosopher of all time to understand. His two works, *Phenomenology of Mind* and the *Science of Logic* are two of the most obscure books in the history of philosophy.

Hegel's aim was highly ambitious. He desired to create a philosophical system that would explain both the past and future in a comprehensive way. He wanted to rationally explain how history was operating and where it was going.

Hegel's philosophy was centered in the concept of *Geist*, which includes the concepts of "Spirit" and "Mind." ("Spirit" represents the religious aspect of reality, and "Mind" represents the rational aspect.) For Hegel, all reality is the outworking of *Geist*. The outworking of *Geist* means that the universe is operating in a rational way that is moving the universe in a more positive direction. Absolute idealism is the name for the view that all reality is shaped by "Spirit" or "Mind."

The concept of freedom was important to Hegel. In fact, for Hegel, "The history of the world is none other than the progress of the consciousness of freedom." The progress of freedom can be seen in the eras of history. First, in the ancient empires such as China, India, and Persia, freedom did not exist at all. Only the ruler was free. Second, the ancient Greeks experienced more freedom, although their situation was far from ideal. Third, freedom triumphed with the Protestant Reformation. At this time individual rights were given their proper place. The time since the Reformation has been the working out of the principle of freedom. Interestingly, Hegel viewed his own authoritarian Prussian state as the final stage of societal development.

Hegel is also known for his theories on the dialectical nature of reality. According to Hegel, history is the struggle between different dynamic concepts that claim to be accurate descriptions of reality. This leads to what has been identified as the "thesis/antithesis/synthesis" model for understanding reality. With this approach, a concept (thesis) necessarily brings forth an opposite concept (antithesis). A struggle then emerges between the thesis and the antithesis until a more truthful synthesis emerges. The newly developed synthesis consists of the most truthful parts of the thesis and antithesis. This newly formed synthesis becomes a thesis from which an opposing antithesis is formed. From this comes another synthesis, and the process continues until the "absolute idea" is reached. Once the perfect "absolute idea" is reached, the thesis/antithesis/synthesis process ends. Thus, history is in progress, and each synthesis leads to a better state for humanity.

After Hegel's death a group called the Young Hegelians argued that Hegel was not true to his own philosophy, and they believed they could apply Hegel's core philosophy in a better way. One of these members was **Karl Marx**. Although often critical of Hegel, Marx adopted Hegel's theory of the process of historical development. Marx, however, replaced "Spirit" with "Matter" as the central element in the process. Through his influence on Karl Marx, Hegel's philosophy impacted the course of history in the nineteenth and twentieth centuries.

75

BIG IDEA:

The "will" is the most basic concept for man and nature.

Arthur Schopenhauer (1788–1860) was a German philosopher who became famous for his idea that "will" is the most basic concept for both man and nature. He is also known for promoting an atheistic and pessimistic view of reality.

Schopenhauer was born in Danzig and studied philosophy at Göttingen in 1810 after a failed attempt at medical school. Schopenhauer openly declared that the chief influences on his philosophy were **Plato, Immanuel Kant**, and the *Upanishads* (holy writings of Hinduism). He was very critical of the ideas of **Georg Hegel**. In fact, Hegel's optimistic views about history were viewed by Schopenhauer as the ramblings of a "stupid and clumsy charlatan."

Schopenhauer was the first notable Western philosopher to openly embrace Hindu and Buddhist ideas. His views are found in his most famous work, *The World as Will and Idea*, which contains four books. The first and third are devoted to the World as Idea; the second and fourth are devoted to the World as Will. Book One begins with his declaration that "The world is my idea." Borrowing from Hindu philosophy, he claimed that the world only exists as an idea in relation to consciousness.

Schopenhauer held a pessimistic view of the world. For him, the world was wretched, and human nature was nasty. People live, breed, and then die. Even his mother disliked him because of his gloomy outlook on life. Schopenhauer's big idea was that "will" drives both animate and inanimate objects in the universe. This will, though, which functions somewhat as a force or appetite, is not a positive thing. For humans, the will desires things that make life even more meaningless and full of suffering. As an atheist he did not believe in an afterlife.

Schopenhauer offered two approaches for escaping the slavery of the will and the wretched suffering that he believed was part of this world. The first is the "aesthetic approach" in which a person loses himself in the arts such as drama, architecture, poetry, paintings, and especially music. The natural beauty of the world is also helpful. According to Schopenhauer, the arts and nature can help a person lose himself in the beauty being contemplated.

The second and better approach, though, is the "ascetic approach." With the ascetic approach, a person renounces the world by extreme self-denial and accepts poverty and injury from both himself and others. In doing these things, the ascetic attempts to kill the "will" and escapes the suffering that often comes from worldly attachments and cravings. Some have pointed out that Schopenhauer's philosophy of renunciation of the will is self-contradictory. If a person wills to renounce the world, is this not an act of the will? Also, if this renunciation happens naturally, can it really be said to be a renunciation?

Schopenhauer's views had a great impact on several important people including the musician Robert Wagner and the philosopher **Friedrich Nietzsche**. His views also impacted **Sigmund Freud**. His critics have sometimes asserted that Schopenhauer did not readily apply his theories to his own life. He ate and drank a lot and had a reputation for being greedy and rude. He once pushed an elderly seamstress down some stairs seriously injuring her.

76

ROMANTICISM

BIG IDEA:

Romanticism was a cultural movement that reacted against the Enlightenment's emphasis on reason and science by stressing the subjective and mysterious elements of reality.

Romanticism was a European cultural, artistic, and intellectual movement that arose in the 1790s and lasted until approximately the end of the nineteenth century. It was a reaction against the **Enlightenment** and its overwhelming emphasis on science and reason. Whereas the Enlightenment tended to objectify reality, Romanticism asserted that there were subjective and even mysterious aspects of reality that could not be fully explained or understood by cold human reason.

Romanticism rebelled against the rationality of the Enlightenment by emphasizing human emotions, creativity, and imagination. It stressed individualism and the thrill of seeking out the unknown and unexplained. Romanticism was about appreciating beauty and color. That which was challenging, unknown, and less-traveled was preferred to that which was familiar. Romanticism exalted man's initiative and creative abilities.

Romanticism was inspired by the writings of **Jean-Jacques Rousseau** and the political changes in America and France. Romanticism spawned several authors, composers, and artists including Hugo, Chopin, Fichte, Schelling, **Hegel**, and **Schopenhauer**. Many view **Friedrich Schleiermacher** as the theologian of the Romanticism because of his emphasis on "feeling" and "sense of absolute dependence" in regard to religion.

77

LUDWIG FEUERBACH

BIG IDEA:

The study of religion is the study of man since God is a myth created by humans.

L udwig Feuerbach (1804–1872) was a German philosopher who became famous for his view that the study of religion or theology is really the study of man since God is merely the projection of human ideals on an imaginary being.

Feuerbach was a student of **Georg Hegel** but eventually rejected much of Hegel's views. Feuerbach substituted Hegel's **idealism** with materialism and believed that people's material needs should be the basis for social and political theory. In his early career Feuerbach studied Protestant theology, but his **worldview** was that of naturalistic humanism. Feuerbach did not believe in the existence of God or the afterlife. In his work *Thoughts on Death and Immortality*, he argued against personal immortality.

Feuerbach is most famous for his assertion that the study of religion is really the study of anthropology (the study of man). According to him, religion reveals how humans project their ideals on an alleged God who really does not exist. Thus, religion teaches us more about humans than God. The study of religion is important, not because it teaches us about God and spiritual truths, but because it helps us understand the nature and essence of people.

For example, the qualities of intelligence, power, goodness, and purity are all things to which humans aspire. But because humans have an idea of a perfect standard and understand that they themselves are less than perfect, they project these qualities upon an imaginary being. This projection, though, gives people an excuse for their imperfections since God is viewed as perfect and humans see themselves as frail and weak. This perspective, however, keeps people in bondage. Instead of trying to improve themselves, people passively accept their imperfections or merely rely on God's grace to help them. Either way, people are not actively striving to better themselves.

For Feuerbach, the major thrust of **philosophy** should be to liberate people from the illusions of religion. He argued for the dissolution of Protestantism so that a more ideal democratic-republican state could be established. Feuerbach's ideas greatly influenced future anti-theist philosophers including **Friedrich Nietzsche** and **Karl Marx**.

78

UTILITARIANISM

BIG IDEA:

What is right or good is that which brings the most happiness for the most people.

U tilitarianism is an ethical theory that declares that what is right or good is that which brings the greatest happiness for the most people. The two founders of utilitarianism are Jeremy Bentham (1748–1832) and **John Stuart Mill** (1806–1873).

With utilitarianism, the focus is upon the potential *consequences* of an action. When faced with a dilemma in which there are two or more choices, utilitarianism instructs us to choose the course of action that would produce the greatest happiness for the most people. Utilitarianism is often viewed as a form of **hedonism** since the emphasis of this view is on happiness and pleasure. Bentham argued that humans are pain and pleasure beings.

Many have been drawn to this approach since it coincides with democratic principles in which the overall will and good of the majority is given high consideration.

Utilitarianism has come under criticism. Some have argued that it is difficult to measure happiness. Plus, it is also difficult to measure the happiness of different groups. Another criticism of utilitarianism is that it is often difficult to predict the consequences of an action. We may choose a course of action that we think will bring the greatest happiness to the most people, but our predictions could be wrong. What if we think a potential action is best but it ends up being a disaster?

Lastly, some have expressed concern that utilitarianism can be used to justify actions that are usually considered immoral. What if hanging an innocent man would greatly deter crime in a society? Mill worried that utilitarianism had the potential to lead to the "tyranny of the majority" in which the rights of minority groups could be trampled for the alleged "good" of the majority. He attempted to put forth a utilitarian approach that respected the rights of minorities and encouraged tolerance of minority groups and views.

79

JOHN STUART MILL

BIG IDEA:

Utilitarianism should emphasize the distinction between "lower" and "higher" pleasures.

John Stuart Mill (1806–1873) was a British philosopher and economist who is often known as a co-founder of **utilitarianism**. He developed the concept of utilitarianism that Jeremy Bentham had started a generation earlier. In fact, Mill's father, James Mill, was a disciple of Bentham.

Mill was brilliant from his youth. Under the instruction of his philosopher father, James Mill, he began studying Greek at age three, and by age seventeen he completed advanced studies of Greek civilization, chemistry, philosophy, psychology, and law. Such learning did not come without a price. John's father often kept him away from other children, and the only recreation he participated in was a daily walk with his father.

Like Bentham, John Stuart Mill promoted the utilitarian view that actions were right and true if they made living conditions better for most people. Mill, though, modified Bentham's utilitarianism. While agreeing in general with Bentham's views, Mill was afraid that Bentham's utilitarianism could lead to the "tyranny of the majority" in which minority groups would be susceptible to persecution by the majority. For example, if the majority decided that gypsies were bad for society, gypsies could be subject to persecution. Mill did not want this. Mill, therefore, made provision for individual freedom and argued that minority groups should be protected from majority oppression. Mill believed that a pluralistic society was good and that all ideas should be heard.

Mill also went further than Bentham by dividing pleasures into "lower" and "higher" pleasures. As Mill once stated, "Some kinds of pleasure are more desirable and more valuable than others." The higher pleasures were things like intellectual, aesthetic, literary, and philosophical pursuits.

Mill had a great impact on English society. He fought for the rights of women including their right to vote. He also advocated equal educational opportunities for women. In line with his utilitarianism, Mill thought bringing equality to women would help society in general.

In 1824, Mill was arrested for distributing birth control information to the London poor. He shared the fears of Malthus (1766–1834), a clergyman who warned that human population would grow faster than human means of production of food. Thus, people should practice either sexual abstinence or birth control.

80

BIG IDEA:

To make life meaningful, you must take a "leap of faith" and passionately believe in something, even though there is no certainty that your belief is true.

Søren Kierkegaard (1813–1855) was a Danish religious philosopher who by stressing individual freedom and the subjective nature of truth became known as the "father of **existentialism**."

Kierkegaard was heavily influenced by events in his early life. He grew up in a strict Lutheran environment, and his mother died when he was young as did five of his six elder siblings. Racked by guilt, Kierkegaard believed that those closest to him were doomed to disaster. That is partly why he broke off his engagement with the love of his life, Regine Olsen. The breakup deeply affected him the rest of his life. When she married someone else, Kierkegaard became bitter and began to dislike all women. His life ended in isolation.

In regard to philosophy, Kierkegaard was interested in freedom and individual existence. He held that people have many life options to choose from, but they must decide for themselves which path to commit to. Thus, he advocated the "leap of faith" in which a person makes a passionate commitment to something without having objective certainty about it. For Kierkegaard, the "leap of faith" was a passionate choice to believe in the Christian God apart from evidence that this God existed. This concept of the "leap of faith" is akin to fideism, which is belief in something apart from reason or rational proofs.

Kierkegaard argued that each person can choose three lifestyles: (1) the aesthetic – the life of pleasure; (2) the ethical – the life of duty, laws, and making decisions; or (3) the religious – the life of service to God. Kierkegaard chose the third option. The leap of faith is necessary to get from the second to the third lifestyle. To illustrate the religious lifestyle, Kierkegaard used the example of the Old Testament patriarch Abraham. According to Kierkegaard, many laud Abraham as the "father of faith" but do not seriously consider that Abraham was willing to kill his own son, Isaac. Abraham was willing to forsake the normal laws of human conduct to obey God in a radical way. The lesson, thus, is that your personal interaction with God is more important than pre-established expectations.

81

EXISTENTIALISM

BIG IDEA:

People face a difficult world alone, but they must passionately choose to believe in something even though they cannot know that their object of faith is true.

Existentialism escapes a simple definition. Generally speaking, though, existentialism is a **philosophy** that emphasizes the uniqueness and isolation of the individual as he or she experiences a hostile and indifferent universe. Common themes within existentialism are individual existence, freedom, uncertainty, subjectivity, responsibility, and choice. Existentialism addresses the nature and purpose of human existence.

Unlike other philosophical systems that focus on metaphysical issues, existentialism focuses more on how people should practically live. Essential to existentialism is its pessimism regarding the ability to find true knowledge or to know anything with certainty. This uncertain nature of life can lead to "angst" or "dread" and a sense that life is absurd and meaningless.

The solution to doubt, though, is to choose to believe passionately in something whether it be God, a political philosophy, or something else. This passionate commitment to something is what gives meaning to life. You may not know for sure that your belief system or your object of belief is correct, but you need to follow it passionately anyway.

Also linked to existentialism is the view that truth is subjective. Truth is related to the individual and not to some universal objective standard. As the founder of existentialism, Søren Kierkegaard stated, "The thing is to find a truth which is true for me, to find the idea for which I can live and die."

Existentialists strongly advocate that individuals have the freedom to choose their own way. Humans are not simply beings who act according to a predetermined nature. It is the choices people make that determine their nature. As existentialist philosopher **Jean-Paul Sartre** stated, "Existence precedes essence." By this he means that we are all thrown into existence first without a predetermined nature. Only later do we construct our nature and who we are through our actions.

Existentialism can be applied broadly. **Søren Kierkegaard** applied it to **Christianity** and **ethics** while Sartre tried to combine existentialism with Marxism and **atheism**. In addition to Kierkegaard and Sartre, other notable existentialist philosophers include Martin Heidegger, Karl Jaspers, and **Simone de Beauvoir**.

82

KARL MARX

BIG IDEA:

Unstoppable economic factors are at work that will eventually cause the workers of the world to unite and overthrow the system of capitalism, and then a classless communist society will begin.

Karl Marx (1818–1883) was a German philosopher, economist, and social theorist who laid the philosophical groundwork for communism. He was born into a Jewish family, but his father insisted that they convert to Protestantism to avoid persecution. In contrast to more abstract philosophers, Marx believed that **philosophy** should actually make a practical difference in people's lives. As he stated, "The philosophers have only interpreted the world, in various ways; the point is to change it."

Marx's views on the eventual triumph of communism were rooted in the dialectical approach of **Georg Hegel** in which history is viewed as a continual struggle between a thesis and antithesis, which eventually leads to a new synthesis. How does this theory work in regard to Marx? Marx viewed human history as a struggle between two great classes. The first class is the *bourgeoisie* (thesis), which consists of those in control of the economic forces. These are the owners of industry including the factories and businesses. The second class is the *proletariat* (antithesis), which consists of the wage-earning workers. According to Marx, the *bourgeoisie* oppress the *proletariat*, but this situation would not always occur. Eventually, through inevitable economic forces, the working class would rise up and overthrow their *bourgeoisie* oppressors. This overthrow would involve a new synthesis in which the workers would control the means of production and equally share goods and services. This new state for humanity will be communism.

This inevitable march toward communism, according to Marx, can be seen in the outworking of history. At first there was slavery, which eventually gave way to feudalism. The feudalism of the Medieval Era eventually gave way to capitalism. Although capitalism has brought some good, like increased production, it is inherently unstable since the vast majority of workers who support this system are mistreated and dehumanized. Within capitalism, the workers are slaves of the *bourgeoisie* in that they are not paid sufficiently or recognized for their work. The workers make the owners of industry rich while they themselves are oppressed and poor. Eventually, though, the working class will get stronger until they revolt and overthrow the *bourgeoisie*. Capitalism, then, will give way to the "dictatorship of the proletariat," and a classless society will appear.

Marx's theory is referred to as "dialectical materialism." Unlike Hegel, who stressed *Geist* ("Spirit" or "Mind") as the controlling factor in history, Marx stressed economic factors as the driving forces in history. *Das Kapital* was Marx's explanation of economics. In 1848, Marx worked with Friedrich Engels to publish the *Communist Manifesto*. The end of the manifesto declares: "The proletarians have nothing to lose but their chains. They have a world to win. Working men of all countries, unite!"

Marx was convinced that the economic and social forces of history would lead to the overthrow of capitalism. But with the decreasing number of communist nations and the dissolution of the Soviet Union at the end of the twentieth century, some have declared that Marx's theory is on the verge of extinction.

83

PRAGMATISM

BIG IDEA:

*Truth is that which is
practical and useful.*

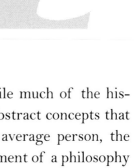

I s truth theoretical or practical? While much of the history of **philosophy** has focused on abstract concepts that appear to have little benefit to the average person, the nineteenth century witnessed the development of a philosophy that was geared toward that which was practical. Pragmatism is a philosophical approach that interprets truth based upon practical effects.

According to pragmatism, truth is what is practical and useful. Thus, something is deemed "true" if it works and "untrue" if it does not work. As a result, the enterprise of philosophy is not just an intellectual or conceptual matter, it should be practical.

Pragmatism is one of the few philosophical concepts that originated in the United States. It is especially linked with the views of C. S. Peirce (1839–1914), William James (1842–1910), and John Dewey (1859–1952).

Pragmatists often view metaphysical speculations as irrelevant since they bring no practical benefits. William James, though, was an exception since he believed pragmatism was consistent with the concepts of God and immortality.

84

EVOLUTION

BIG IDEA:

Humans developed from primitive beginnings over a long period of time, thus, the origin and development of humans can be attributed to purely natural means.

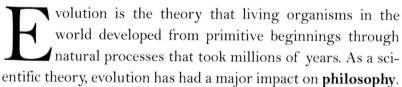

volution is the theory that living organisms in the world developed from primitive beginnings through natural processes that took millions of years. As a scientific theory, evolution has had a major impact on **philosophy**.

While many view the theory of evolution as a nineteenth-century phenomenon, several philosophers in the Pre-Socratic Era of ancient Greece promoted forms of evolution. Anaximander (611–547 B.C.), for example, held that people evolved from fish. He believed this so strongly that he encouraged people not to eat fish since they were our ancestors.

Empedocles (490–430 B.C.), too, believed in a form of evolution when he declared that random chance formed matter into isolated limbs. For example, there once were arms without shoulders, heads without necks, and eyes without eye sockets. These parts eventually linked into organisms in which there were beings like human-headed oxen and ox-headed humans. Only the fittest of these beings survived.

The early nineteenth century Frenchman, Jean-Baptiste de Lamarck, became the first to offer a detailed explanation of evolution. However, the English naturalist, Charles Darwin, is most associated with the theory of evolution. His thoughts on evolution developed as a result of his five-year tour of the globe on the HMS *Beagle*. His two landmark works that launched the theory of evolution were *The Origin of Species* (1859) and *The Descent of Man* (1871). According to Darwin, organisms vary based on their ability to adapt to their environments. Organisms evolve gradually to help them adapt to their surroundings. The fittest of species adapt and survive while weaker organisms do not live.

Evolution has had enormous philosophical implications. While it does not necessarily rule out the existence of God, it does offer a view of origins that is purely naturalistic and does not rely on the supernatural. Many atheists and secular humanists, therefore, have been attracted to evolution since it explains reality apart from any divine being. Before Darwin's view of evolution, the Western world generally accepted the Genesis account in the Bible concerning the creation of the world in six literal days.

Darwin's theory challenged other traditional beliefs including the perspective that the world was only a few thousand years old. With Darwin's theory, millions of years are necessary since the gradual changes in species occur over long periods of time. Darwin's view also challenged the traditional belief that people were made in the image of God and, thus, were radically different and superior to all other beings in the world.

Evolution is a widely accepted theory today, but it is not held by all scholars. While acknowledging that micro-evolution takes place within species, some have argued that irreducibly complex aspects of certain species rule out the possibility of macro-evolution as posited by Darwin.

85

FRIEDRICH NIETZSCHE

BIG IDEA:

God is dead to modern man,
so humankind needs to construct
a new morality.

Friedrich Nietzsche (1844–1900) was a famous German philosopher of the late nineteenth century. The son of a Lutheran pastor, Nietzsche studied at the University of Leipzig where, in 1865, he was attracted to the atheistic beliefs of another German philosopher—**Arthur Schopenhauer**. From this point onward, Nietzsche became an opponent of **Christianity**. In addition to Schopenhauer, early influences on Nietzsche included Darwin's theory of **evolution** and the German composer Robert Wagner (Nietzsche rejected Wagner, though, when Wagner became a Christian).

Nietzsche questioned the traditional intellectual and moral foundation of Western civilization and launched an aggressive attack on Christianity. He believed that the values and ideas of traditional Christianity had lost their power. While Christianity may have had some benefit for ancient societies, it no longer served our modern world well and needed to be replaced.

Nietzsche was the first to coin the phrase "God is dead," which means that the traditional views of God and morality have no meaning or value for today. He also argued that Christianity created a "slave morality" in which people were convinced to be weak under the guise of kindness. He called on people to reject the "morality of the herd" and to stop being stupid followers of old beliefs.

For Nietzsche, new values needed to replace old ones. The person who could rise above the old and outmoded beliefs could rise to the level of a "superman." The superman (*ubermensch*) is the one who puts aside the herd mentality and has the "will to power"—the will to live in a more powerful state. The superman also focuses on the current life and not some alleged afterlife.

Nietzsche argued that the world was the result of random chance and that humans, like animals, were just a part of nature. Also, the world has no purpose. For Nietzsche, there is no objective or universal truth. Philosophy, religion, metaphysics, and science have failed to prove that there are absolute truths or absolute knowledge. These particular ideas have caused many in recent years to identify Nietzsche as the "father of **postmodernism**," although postmodernism did not begin for another sixty years.

The Nazis viewed Nietzsche as a precursor of their ideas, but it is probably not fair to label Nietzsche as a Nazi even though his ideas were influential on them. During his life,

Nietzsche was plagued by poor eyesight and migraine head-aches. By 1889, he started to show signs of insanity, and he lived in senile retirement under the care of his sister. He died in 1900.

86

NIHILISM

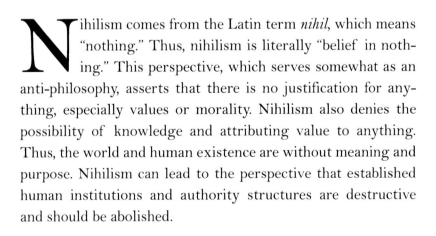

BIG IDEA:

Human existence is without meaning and purpose.

Nihilism comes from the Latin term *nihil*, which means "nothing." Thus, nihilism is literally "belief in nothing." This perspective, which serves somewhat as an anti-philosophy, asserts that there is no justification for anything, especially values or morality. Nihilism also denies the possibility of knowledge and attributing value to anything. Thus, the world and human existence are without meaning and purpose. Nihilism can lead to the perspective that established human institutions and authority structures are destructive and should be abolished.

The term "nihilism" was first used in 1862 by Ivan Turgenev in his novel *Father and Sons* to describe young rebels in Russia. Some **Sophists** of ancient Greece, who believed truth and morals were relative, held nihilistic beliefs.

Nihilism is often associated with the philosophy of **Friedrich Nietzsche** who argued strongly for the overthrow of the morality and values of the Judeo-Christian tradition. Nihilism is also linked with twentieth-century movements such as deconstructionism and **postmodernism**.

By definition, nihilism is belief in nothing, but since nihilism is asserting a belief ("belief in nothing"), it could be argued that nihilism is inherently contradictory. Perhaps nihilism is best understood in the context of challenging established morality and belief systems and not as an independent philosophy of its own.

87

SIGMUND FREUD

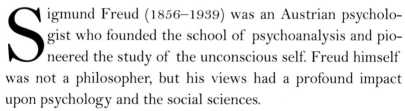

BIG IDEA:

Each person is heavily influenced by a powerful unconscious self.

Sigmund Freud (1856–1939) was an Austrian psychologist who founded the school of psychoanalysis and pioneered the study of the unconscious self. Freud himself was not a philosopher, but his views had a profound impact upon psychology and the social sciences.

Freud viewed the self as a multi-tiered entity consisting of both the conscious and unconscious realms. Consciousness refers to the mental thoughts of which we are aware. Unconsciousness, on the other hand, refers to the mental processes of which we are usually not aware. The study of the conscious self was nothing new, but it was Freud's treatment of the unconscious that made him famous.

According to Freud, our unconscious self is the dominating influence in our lives, affecting how we act and think. It contains all of our basic and primal instincts including sexuality, aggressiveness, and our bent toward self-destruction and death. These primal desires always seek instant gratification or release. According to Freud, these primal instincts need to be channeled in an appropriate way or neurotic behavior will ensue. Our conscious self, on the other hand, operates according to the "reality principle" and tries to control our unconscious self. The aim of our conscious self is to help us act rationally and appropriately so that we can function practically and in harmony with our social environment.

For Freud, the unconscious self reveals itself in three main ways. First, it shows itself in slips of the tongue or "Freudian slips." These occur when you unexpectedly say what you *really thought* instead of what you *intended* to say. For example, you tell someone "I thought you did an *awful* job on your project" when you intended to say "I thought you did an *awesome* job." Second, the unconscious self also reveals itself in dreams. Third, the clearest expressions of the unconscious, according to Freud, occur when a person evidences neurotic behavior such as continually washing one's hands or being chronically depressed.

Freud is known for stressing the importance of sexuality and infancy to mental health. He promoted the theory that young boys have sexual desires for their mothers, but the fathers of each boy repress these desires, and the boys recoil for fear of being castrated by their fathers. For Freud, such suppression of infantile sexual desires is the root of neurotic behavior in adults.

Many of Freud's ideas have been rejected and replaced but his influence in the field of psychoanalysis is unquestioned.

88

BERTRAND RUSSELL

BIG IDEA:

Mathematical truths can be translated into truths of logic.

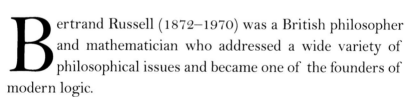

Bertrand Russell (1872–1970) was a British philosopher and mathematician who addressed a wide variety of philosophical issues and became one of the founders of modern logic.

Russell invented "philosophical logic," which was not so much a **philosophy** as it was a method or approach to philosophy. He also approached math philosophically by claiming that mathematical truths can be translated into truths of logic. In his book, *Principles of Mathematics*, Russell argued that mathematics is simply logic.

In regard to **epistemology** and **metaphysics**, Russell developed the concept of "logical atomism" in which thought and discourse are analyzed in terms of indivisible parts or atomic propositions. Atomic propositions are true if they correspond with atomic facts. An atomic fact is the most basic kind of fact that can be expressed in a simple sentence with no connectives. An example of an atomic proposition would be "The ball is blue."

An ardent atheist, Russell set forth his arguments against the existence of God in his essay "Why I Am Not a Christian." He attempted to refute the "first cause argument" (or **cosmological argument**) for God's existence by stating that if everything needs a cause, what caused God? For Russell, if it must be assumed that something is not caused, why not believe that the world is eternal and not God? Russell also rejected the "argument from design" (or **teleological argument**) claiming that the presence of groups like the Ku Klux Klan and fascists makes it unlikely that a good God created the world.

In his later years, Russell focused his efforts on humanitarian issues like nuclear disarmament. In his work *Fly and the Fly-Bottle*, he declared, "Why waste time on philosophy when mankind is in danger of destroying itself?" Twice he was arrested for his involvement with anti-nuclear protests. Russell was a candidate for Parliament on three occasions but was defeated each time. He was awarded the Nobel Prize for Literature in 1950. His work *A History of Western Philosophy* became a standard text in philosophy courses at universities for several decades. His most famous student was **Ludwig Wittgenstein**, who studied under Russell at Cambridge University.

Russell's parents died when he was young, and he was brought up by his grandmother. She had him privately tutored until he was ready to attend Cambridge University where he majored in mathematics and philosophy. He married four times; the first three marriages ended in divorce.

89

LUDWIG WITTGENSTEIN

BIG IDEA:

Words are tools that serve many functions, but they do not have inherent meanings of their own.

T he son of a wealthy industrialist, Ludwig Wittgenstein (1889–1951) was an Austrian philosopher who became one of the most important philosophers of the twentieth century.

Born in Vienna, Wittgenstein studied mechanical engineering in Berlin (1906–1908) and in Manchester, England (1908–1911). Then he moved to Cambridge University to study mathematical logic under **Bertrand Russell** (1912–1913). After that he served as an artillery officer on the German-Austrian side.

In 1922, Wittgenstein wrote his *Tractatus Logico-philosophicus*, a work that he believed was the "final solution" to philosophical problems. In this work Wittgenstein promoted the "picture theory" of language in which words represent things according to established conventions.

After writing the *Tractatus*, Wittgenstein gave away his money and worked as an elementary school teacher in country districts in Austria from 1920 to 1926. He also worked as a gardener's assistant in a monastery and designed and built a building. He finally returned to Cambridge University in 1929 after a sixteen-year absence and stayed there until he resigned his professorship in 1947.

When he returned to philosophy, he rejected his views in the *Tractatus* including his picture theory. He asserted that usage was more important than convention. For Wittgenstein, words are like "tools" that serve many functions. He also asserted that there are no inherent meanings in words and that the meaning of a word is determined by how a person uses that word (i.e., context).

Wittgenstein is famous for his idea of "language games" by which he means that people play different games with language. For example, the scientist uses the language of a scientist, and the theologian uses the language of theologian. In order to understand scientists and theologians, you need to learn the words they use, and thus, play their language games.

Wittgenstein died of cancer in 1951. His ideas from his later period were published after his death as the *Philosophical Investigations* in 1953.

90

LOGICAL POSITIVISM

BIG IDEA:

Only statements that can be verified scientifically are genuine; all other statements are meaningless.

L ogical positivism was a scientifically oriented philo-sophical movement that arose in the early part of the twentieth century. Its main assertion was that only statements that could be verified empirically are genuine. All other statements are meaningless.

Logical positivism tried to link **philosophy** with sci-ence. It had its roots in the empirical skepticism of **David Hume**. More directly, though, logical positivism arose in the early twentieth century from a group of teachers and stu-dents from the University of Vienna. This "Vienna Circle," as it came to be called, consisted of several scientists who wanted to develop a modern and scientific philosophy that would sweep away many of the problems of **metaphysics** and religion. Logical positivism gained ground steadily, but it became a major force when A. J. Ayer wrote his *Language, Truth, and Logic* in 1936. This work launched a major assault on metaphysics.

At its heart, logical positivism can rightly be regarded as an anti-metaphysical philosophy. As its chief weapon, logical positivists used the verification principle. The verification principle is a principle that distinguishes genuine factual statements from meaningless statements. According to logical positivists, the purpose of language is to make statements about the world and to communicate experiences.

Essential to logical positivism, therefore, is the belief that only empirically verifiable statements are genuine. This philosophy had a negative perspective toward the metaphysical truth claims of religion and **Christianity** in particular. For logical positivists, theologians may speak of God's existence, the soul, and immortality as factual matters, but these matters cannot be put to empirical and scientific observation. Thus, any statements about these things are meaningless. In fact, whenever anyone makes factual assertions about matters such as God, the soul, and immortality, they are really making meaningless emotional assertions.

Logical positivism should be distinguished from **atheism**. Atheism claims that religious assertions about God are false, while logical positivism argues that they are meaningless. Logical positivism was initially well received by those interested in a modern philosophy that was scientifically based. The Austrian philosopher **Ludwig Wittgenstein** shared an approach similar to that of the logical positivists. Eventually, though, people began to question logical positivism. Since the verification principle itself could not be verified empirically, many concluded that logical positivism was internally contradictory. After World War II logical positivism came under attack, and by the late 1960s the movement collapsed.

91

EMOTIVISM

BIG IDEA:

All ethical statements are expressions of emotion and, thus, are meaningless.

Emotivism is a philosophical theory in the realm of **ethics**. It is the view that all ethical statements are expressions of emotion and, thus, are meaningless. For example, statements such as "Abortion is wrong" or "Euthanasia is okay" are emotional opinions that relate solely to how a person feels about a certain issue. With emotivism, ethical statements are emotional attempts to get others to agree with one's views.

As a result, emotivism is sometimes referred to as the "Boo/Hooray" theory. It is as if you are saying "Boo" when you disagree with an ethical position, and you are cheering "Hooray" when you agree with a view.

Critics of emotivism have said that if this perspective is taken seriously, then there can be no meaningful discussion about ethics. Critics also say that this view is potentially dangerous because if accepted, serious ethical issues will be trivialized. Plus, it has been argued that emotivism leaves us with no objective way to analyze ethical matters.

Some have seen the foundation for emotivism in the writings of **David Hume**. Emotivism, though, came to prominence in the 1930s with the teachings of A. J. Ayer. His book *Language, Truth and Logic* is often viewed as containing the classical presentation of emotivism.

92

KARL POPPER

BIG IDEA:

Scientific theories should always be subject to falsification.

Karl Popper (1902–1994) was an Austrian-born British philosopher who argued that scientific theories should continually be subject to falsification.

In *The Logic of Scientific Discovery*, Popper challenged the view that **induction**, as applied to the scientific realm, could lead to certain conclusions. Instead, scientific observations and theories should always be subject to falsification. This means that when establishing a theory, the scientist should always be on the lookout for any data that would falsify his or her own theory. If falsifying data is found, then the theory must be rejected or modified to fit the new data. If falsifying data is not found, the theory should be accepted, at least for a time, knowing that data in the future may falsify the theory.

Popper's approach makes the theories of science less certain and open to potential falsification in the future. For instance, an inductive study may lead us to conclude that all swans are white because that is what our observations have indicated. However, we should be open to the possibility that someday we might discover a swan that is not white. If this occurs, then we must jettison or modify the theory that "all swans are white." But for now we can act upon the assumption that all swans are white.

Some have claimed that Popper's theory is similar to that of **David Hume**, who challenged traditional views of cause and effect. Others have complained that Popper's view leads to an approach in which the main goal of science is simply to disprove established theories. If this is the case, does this mean there are no theories we can act upon? Popper, though, did believe that some theories have survived critical testing and, thus, are worthy to be acted upon.

In his early career, Popper was associated with the logical positivists, a group of scholars who were negative about metaphysical knowledge. Popper, however, never held that metaphysical and nonscientific matters were meaningless.

In *The Open Society and Its Enemies*, Popper addressed political philosophy. He advocated open societies and defended democracy. He also offered objections to the totalitarian views of **Plato** and **Karl Marx**. Popper left Vienna for New Zealand in 1937 because of the threat of Nazi occupation of Austria. He taught at Canterbury University, New Zealand, from 1937 to 1945. Later, he was a professor at the University of London. Popper was knighted by Queen Elizabeth II in 1965 and was known as Sir Karl for the rest of his life.

93

JEAN-PAUL SARTRE

BIG IDEA:

"Existence precedes essence" since people have the freedom to choose what kind of a person they will be.

Jean-Paul Sartre (1905–1980) was a French author, playwright, political theorist, and literary critic who became famous for his promotion of atheistic existentialism. Along with **Søren Kierkegaard** (1813–1855), Sartre is viewed as one of the primary promoters of **existentialism**.

Sartre believed that striving to be an authentic individual was the most important thing in life. Living the authentic life means understanding that we are "condemned to be free." According to Sartre, human beings are completely free and responsible for every decision and action they take in life. There is no God or predetermined nature that determines who people are.

This belief led to his declaration that "existence precedes essence," which means that a person appears on the scene first (existence) and then chooses what he or she will become (essence). For Sartre, the first principle of existentialism is this: "Man is nothing else but what he makes of himself." Thus, the task of existentialism is to make people understand that they are responsible for their own existence.

The responsibility that Sartre calls for does not just involve the individual person—it also involves the human race. Whenever a person makes a choice, which contributes to who he is as a person, he is also choosing for everyone else. How is this so? According to Sartre, when you make a decision, you not only define yourself, but you implicitly make a statement concerning how other human beings should act. As Sartre stated, "In choosing myself, I choose man."

This approach is similar to Immanuel Kant's **categorical imperative** in which a person is encouraged to act in such a way that, if possible, his action could become a universal law for others. Thus, Sartre believed that the actions of a person define not only him but the human race as well. For example, Sartre believed that when a man chooses to marry a woman and have children, he involves all mankind in monogamy, not just himself.

In a manner similar to **Socrates**, Sartre also believed that people never do evil intentionally. If they do, it is because of ignorance, and if enlightened, they will choose the good every time because that is always in their best interest.

Sartre was extremely popular in France because of his plays and novels. During World War II he was a fighter for the French Resistance and was captured by the Nazis. Sartre rejected the Nobel Peace Prize in 1964 because he said accepting it would jeopardize his integrity as a writer. Sartre was also sympathetic to the communism of the Soviet Union and is famous for his love affair with the feminist and fellow existentialist philosopher **Simone de Beauvoir**.

94

AYN RAND

BIG IDEA:

*Seeking one's self-interests first
is a good thing and should be
acknowledged and accepted by society.*

Ayn Rand (1905–1982) was an American novelist and philosopher who promoted a form of **ethical egoism** in which a person should always act according to his or her self-interests.

According to Rand, the primary function of morality should be to further our evolutionary survival. She strongly rejected the prevailing view of altruism in which selfishness is considered evil and the highest good is that of putting the needs of others above oneself. For Rand, altruism asks people to adopt an ethic that goes against their natural and primal impulses to survive. It also discourages people from seeking their full potential and greatness. Thus, the old morality should be replaced with a new morality that recognizes the need for people to act in their own interests first.

Rand's emphasis on self-interest is not a call for reckless **hedonism** in which a person simply acts on any desires he or she may have. One's self-interests must be rational. Thus, a person should rationally pursue his or her self-interests in a way that is not destructive to one's being. For example, the desire to abuse alcohol or drugs would not be valid according to Rand because these lead to destruction and are not in the best interest of the individual. Rand's approach also does not lead to a negative perspective toward other people. Others are not enemies, and individuals should have cordial and productive relationships with other people while knowing all along that one's interests supersede those of others.

Also a screenwriter and playwright, Rand was one of the leading female philosophers of the twentieth century, Rand is known for two famous fictional books—*The Fountainhead* (1943) and *Atlas Shrugged* (1957). She was born in Saint Petersburg in tsarist Russia and immigrated to the United States in 1926. An atheist, Rand argued against political states that sponsored communism and fascism.

95

SIMONE DE BEAUVOIR

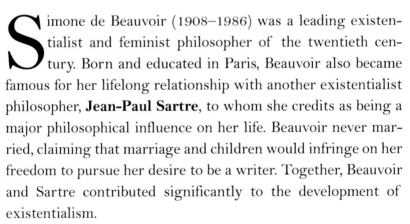

BIG IDEA:

Women need to realize that they are free to determine their own destinies.

S imone de Beauvoir (1908–1986) was a leading existentialist and feminist philosopher of the twentieth century. Born and educated in Paris, Beauvoir also became famous for her lifelong relationship with another existentialist philosopher, **Jean-Paul Sartre**, to whom she credits as being a major philosophical influence on her life. Beauvoir never married, claiming that marriage and children would infringe on her freedom to pursue her desire to be a writer. Together, Beauvoir and Sartre contributed significantly to the development of existentialism.

In her book *The Second Sex*, Beauvoir surveyed the history of male oppression throughout history and discussed how the female sex has often been portrayed as the "other" sex by males. A predominant theme in her writings is freedom. In line with existentialist thought, Beauvoir argued that people have the right to create their own existence. This includes women, who should not just passively accept the stereotypical roles that Western society has placed upon them.

According to her, women themselves have been largely responsible for the oppression they have received. Interestingly, she argued that being female is a matter of choice and not biology. "One is not born, but rather becomes a woman," she declared.

Along with Sartre and a few others, she was the editor of the socialist magazine *Les Temps modernes*. She was one of the leading feminists of her era.

96

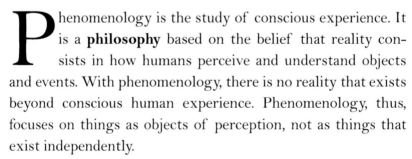

BIG IDEA:

Reality consists in how humans perceive objects and events.

P henomenology is the study of conscious experience. It is a **philosophy** based on the belief that reality consists in how humans perceive and understand objects and events. With phenomenology, there is no reality that exists beyond conscious human experience. Phenomenology, thus, focuses on things as objects of perception, not as things that exist independently.

Phenomenology is one of the most important philosophical movements of the twentieth century. It began with the teachings of the Austrian philosopher Edmund Husserl (1859–1938) who used the term "phenomenology" in his work *Ideas: A General Introduction to Pure Phenomenology*. In *Logical*

Investigations (1901), Husserl stated that we should focus on objects as they are presented in actual perception. As used by Husserl, "phenomenology" functions as a principle of philosophical and scientific method. According to Husserl, the mind can contemplate nonexistent things as well as real objects.

Thus, phenomenology does not presuppose that anything exists. Instead, there needs to be a "bracketing" of existence in which we set aside the issue of the real existence of objects. With bracketing, we should not discuss things like trees and rocks as objects external to our experience. Instead, we should discuss objects like these as perceptions of experience. Our focus should be on our experience and not on objects as they are in themselves.

Unlike positivism, phenomenology views reality as basically subjective and relative. It also does not rely exclusively upon empirical data but relies equally upon mental processes.

Phenomenologists do not think there are fundamental levels of reality beyond human conscious experience. They also claim that the reasons for human behavior are to be found within the field of human experience alone and not phenomena outside of human experience. In addition, phenomenologists believe that the mind and body of a person are unified and not separate. Thus, the self is a unity with the mental and physical woven together.

Phenomenology has been very influential in the areas of psychology and the social sciences.

97

JOHN RAWLS

BIG IDEA:

Society should operate on the principles of fairness and equal rights.

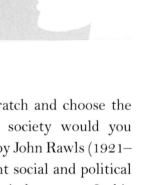

If you could somehow start from scratch and choose the society you wanted, what type of society would you choose? This question was proposed by John Rawls (1921–2002), who was one of the most important social and political philosophers of the last half of the twentieth century. In his most significant work, *A Theory of Justice* (1972), he promoted a political philosophy based on the concept of "justice as fairness" in which justice is necessarily linked to fairness.

In promoting his theory of the ideal state, Rawls relied partly upon the social contract theory of **Thomas Hobbes** and **John Locke** in which people allegedly enter into a contract with each other to promote their own survival and good.

But instead of speculating about what societal contract people actually entered into in the past, Rawls argued that we should focus on the type of contract we would want to enter into now. Thus, if we could somehow start from scratch and choose our ideal society, what standards and criteria would we choose to create this society?

Rawls said we should begin with what he calls "The Veil of Ignorance." The Veil of Ignorance assumes that no person will know who he or she will be in this new society. Before the society actually begins, all factors such as race, gender, age, talents, intelligence, education, and parents are totally hidden. Under this Veil of Ignorance, which type of society would the people choose? Rawls argues that most people would choose a society in which equality and fairness were the rule. After all, what sane person would want to take a chance on receiving unequal and unfair treatment in life? For example, a person probably would not choose a society in which slavery existed or women were given lesser rights if there was a chance that he or she might be a slave or a woman in this society.

According to Rawls, the ideal society would operate on two principles. First, each person would have equal rights and access to the most basic liberties. Every person would be eligible to vote or run for office. Each person would have freedom of thought and speech. Every person also would have the right to own property and have freedom from arbitrary arrest.

Second, all people would have equal opportunities in regard to pursuing careers and economic opportunities. Rawls was not arguing for equal distribution of wealth as socialism does; instead, he stated that all people should have equal access to all jobs and economic opportunities. By implication, this would mean equal access to education that would lead to the best jobs and opportunities. Recognizing that people will have different talents and motivations, Rawls acknowledged that some will have more economic wealth than others. This is acceptable, though, as long as the economic inequalities will benefit society.

For example, if because of hard work and intelligence one person obtains more wealth than others, this could be a good thing if the hard work and intelligence which led to that person's wealth benefited society. Thus, Rawls's society rewards excellence while offering benefits to all of society. Rawls also believed that society should have a safety net to ensure a decent quality of life for its members.

Rawls attended Princeton as a student and taught at both Cornell and Harvard.

98

JOHN HICK

BIG IDEA:

All major religions are expressions of one absolute reality and are equal.

John Hick (1922–) is one of the most influential philosophers of religion in the last fifty years. He is known for two primary contributions: (1) espousing religious pluralism and (2) promoting an Irenaean theodicy in regard to the **problem of evil** in the world.

Perhaps more than any other person, Hick has become associated with religious pluralism—the view that there is a single absolute reality that is mediated through various world religions. Hick asserts that all the major religions of the world stand on equal footing when it comes to understanding truth and reality. Thus, no major religion is superior to any other, nor is salvation only to be found in just one religion. Hick argues that the ethical standards of each religion are strikingly similar. He also asserts that equally good people can be found in all religions. For him, this is evidence that no one religion has the corner on the truth.

According to Hick, the different beliefs and practices of the various religions can be attributed to cultural differences and preferences. Hick himself identified with the Christian tradition, but in doing so, admits that he is culturally inclined towards **Christianity** and states that Hindus, Buddhists, Muslims, and adherents of other religions are just as correct for holding to their traditions. Interestingly, Hick denies the divinity of Jesus, asserting that the doctrine of the Incarnation (God becoming man) is a myth. For if Jesus were truly divine this would naturally mean that Christianity was the superior religion.

Hick is also known for promoting a form of the Irenaean theodicy in regard to the problem of evil in the world. Borrowing from the Christian leader, Irenaeus, Hick asserts that God created people with the need for soul-making or personal development. Since a perfect environment would not lead to personal character development, God allowed evil to help people grow spiritually and to prepare them for the better world to follow.

99

JACQUES DERRIDA

BIG IDEA:

There are no objective realities upon which language is based; all interpretations are equally valid with no one "meaning" being superior to any other.

Jacques Derrida (1930–2004) was a French philosopher who became famous for establishing the process of deconstruction in regard to communication. Extremely complicated by nature, Derrida's deconstruction approach is a postmodern philosophy that is negative concerning the ability of language to refer to objective reality outside of itself.

According to Derrida, words never have referents other than other words. For example, a word like *car* points to other words like *vehicle* or *transportation*, but it does not point to some reality outside of language. Derrida, therefore, rejected what he called "logo-centrism"—the belief that there is some stable point outside of language such as reason or revelation. Derrida believed that logo-centrism has wrongly been used as a tool of oppression by those who believe they alone possess the "truth." This can apply to religions, nations, or any group that claims its views are more correct than others.

Derrida's philosophy is extremely complicated, but its implications are significant since, if correct, it overturns conceptions about language and reality that have been held for all of human history.

For Derrida, there is no such thing as "authorial intent" or "single meanings" for texts. Instead, there are as many meanings as there are interpreters. For example, if ten people read the book *The Grapes of Wrath*, they could all come up with different but equally valid interpretations of this book. No one could rightly say, "My interpretation is more correct than yours." Thus, for Derrida, no one meaning is superior to another meaning. One of the purposes of deconstruction is to pick apart texts to show that they do not teach what most people think they do. Derrida himself tried to show how a text can support two mutually exclusive interpretations.

With Derrida's perspective, attempts to view matters objectively are doomed to failure. If correct, Derrida's views are devastating to **philosophy** and religion since both these disciplines deal so heavily with words. For Derrida, philosophers and theologians are in no better position to understand reality than the average person on the street. Thus, Derrida's deconstruction method appears to call into the question the necessity of traditional centers of knowledge including universities and colleges. Yet Derrida's own philosophy seems to undermine the influence of his own writings since Derrida expected others to understand his writings.

Starting in 1967, Derrida wrote a series of three books that set forth his ideas concerning deconstruction—*Speech and Phenomena, Of Grammatology*, and *Writing and Difference*.

100

PLURALISM

BIG IDEA:

*All major religions are equal—
no one religion is superior
to others.*

luralism is a term that can have different emphases. Three are mentioned here. First, there is empirical pluralism, which refers to the growing racial and religious diversity in our culture. Empirical pluralism is a statistical fact since Western society has recently experienced an increased integration of people of different races and religious beliefs.

Second, philosophical pluralism is the view that no ideological belief system is superior to any other. It is often based on the perspective that there is no objective truth that can make one system of thought as being more "right" than others.

Third, religious pluralism is the view that all major religions are equal and that no one religion is superior to another.

Religious pluralism asserts that all religions are different manifestations of the absolute and, thus, are equal when it comes
to understanding truth and obtaining salvation. The primary
promoter of religious pluralism in recent years is **John Hick**.

Religious pluralism differs from both exclusivism and
inclusivism. Exclusivism holds that one religion is superior and
that salvation can only be found in one religion. Traditional
Christianity and Islam are exclusivistic religions. Inclusivism
is the view that one religion is truer than others, but salvation can also be found in other religions. Christian inclusivists,
for example, assert that salvation is ultimately based in Jesus
Christ, but people of other religions can be saved by following
their religions if they have never heard of Christ. The Roman
Catholic Church adopted inclusivism at its Vatican II Council in
the mid-1960s.

101

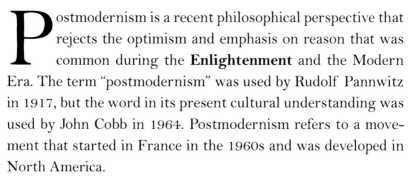

POSTMODERNISM

BIG IDEA:

*Human reason cannot provide
a foundation for knowledge.*

Postmodernism is a recent philosophical perspective that rejects the optimism and emphasis on reason that was common during the **Enlightenment** and the Modern Era. The term "postmodernism" was used by Rudolf Pannwitz in 1917, but the word in its present cultural understanding was used by John Cobb in 1964. Postmodernism refers to a movement that started in France in the 1960s and was developed in North America.

Postmodernism is essentially a negative reaction to the Modern Era and the ideals of the Enlightenment. During the Modern Era (from approximately 1600–1960), Western civilization was basically optimistic about understanding truth and reality. In general, people of this period believed in universal knowledge and truth and held that reason and science could solve most problems. People during this time often disagreed on what the "truth" was, but most believed that "truth" was out there somewhere and could be found.

Postmodernism, though, has challenged these optimistic assumptions in four ways. First, postmodernism is known for its loss of confidence in human reason. In the Postmodern Era many deny that human reason can provide a foundation for true knowledge of the world.

Second, postmodernism rejects the concept of universal, absolute truth. Thus, with postmodernism, there is no God, natural law, or universal standard that determines what is right and wrong. Instead, truth is viewed as relative to individuals and societies.

Third, postmodernism questions the ability of science, education, and technology to solve the major problems of the world. Science, education, and technology are viewed as doing great good, but they are also viewed as having the capacity to bring great harm as well (i.e., a nuclear bomb). Thus, the optimism that accompanied science, technology, and education during the Modern Era has been muted somewhat.

Fourth, postmodernism is sometimes linked with religious pluralism—the view that all religions are equally valid. In the Postmodern Era it is often considered arrogant and intolerant to assert that one's religion or viewpoint is better than or superior to that of others.

Postmodernism is often viewed as a negative movement since it is known more for what it denies than what it affirms. Some believe postmodernism is here to stay while others believe it is already starting to crumble.

RECOMMENDED READING

For more information on philosophy, consider looking at the following works:

Audi, Robert, ed. *The Cambridge Dictionary of Philosophy.* 3rd ed. Cambridge University Press, 2015.

Blackburn, Simon. *Oxford Dictionary of Philosophy.* Oxford: Oxford University Press, 2008.

Honderich, Ted, ed. *The Oxford Companion to Philosophy.* Oxford: Oxford University Press, 1995.

Kenny, Anthony. *A Brief History of Western Philosophy.* Malden, MA: Blackwell, 1998.

Tarnas, Richard. *The Passion of the Western Mind: Understanding the Ideas That Have Shaped Our World View.* New York: Ballantine Books, 1993.

ABOUT THE AUTHOR

Michael J. Vlach, Ph.D. is Professor of Theology at The Master's Seminary in Sun Valley, California where he has been teaching full time since 2006. Michael earned a B.S. in Business Administration from the University of Nebraska and a M.Div. degree from The Master's Seminary in Sun Valley, California. He also earned the Ph.D. in Systematic Theology from Southeastern Baptist Theological Seminary in Wake Forest, North Carolina.

Michael specializes in the areas of Systematic Theology, Historical Theology, Apologetics, and World Religions. His specific area of expertise concerns the nation Israel and issues related to refuting the doctrine of Replacement Theology. Dr. Vlach was awarded the "Franz-Delitzsch Prize 2008" for his dissertation, "The Church as a Replacement of Israel: An Analysis of Supersessionism."

He is also the author of five books, including: *Has the Church Replaced Israel?: A Theological Evaluation* (B & H Academic, 2010), *20 Tips for Writing Seminary Papers* (Theological Studies Press, 2010), and *Dispensationalism: Essential Beliefs and Common Myths* (Theological Studies Press, 2008)

Dr. Vlach is also the Founder and President of TheologicalStudies.org, a cutting-edge website devoted to providing quality articles, news, and information related to Christian theology. Michael speaks regularly at churches and conferences and has appeared on several national radio and television broadcasts including The History Channel.

Michael is also a member of the Evangelical Theological Society and has taught various courses in Theology for Liberty University in Lynchburg, Virginia.

To learn more about Dr. Vlach visit
www.TheologicalStudies.org

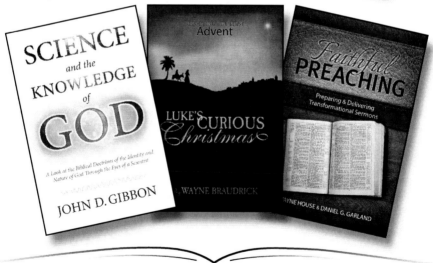